The

Connection

Arthur Bray

Jupiter Publishing,
P.O. Box 5528,
Station "F",
Ottawa, Ontario K2C 3M1
Canada

ISBN 0-9690135-0-7

First Printing 1979

Freedom to Think

Listen to the conversations around you on any given day, and you will hear expressions of the vicarious mind. People will tell you what so-and-so said, or what they read or heard here and there, but only very seldom what they think. And when pressed to explain what they think, they are apt to reveal that they have not really thought much at all. They are expressing not so much thought as opinions, and their opinions are based all too often on third-rate information and analysis.

Amidst the glut of insignificance that engulfs us all, the temptation is understandable to stop thinking. The trouble is that unthinking persons cannot choose but must let others choose for them. But to fail to make one's own choices is to betray the freedom which is our society's greatest gift to all of us.

— From "Notable and Quotable" by Steven Muller,
in the *Wall Street Journal*, January 8, 1979

By the same author

Science, the Public and the UFO

ACKNOWLEDGEMENTS

With any research, there are always those who assist the researcher in many ways. In my case, it would have been impossible to obtain much of my data had it not been for the kind help of many people to whom I am indebted. Among those were Dr. Peter M. Millman, Dr. Allen G. McNamara and Annie Claude of the Planetary Sciences Section, Herzberg Institute of Astrophysics, National Research Council.

In addition to other assistance, Dr. McNamara kindly granted me permission to publish the final report of Project Magnet. Dr. John deMercado of the Department of Communications granted me permission to use material from that department's files on Project Magnet. Dr. Steven Muller, President of Johns Hopkins University, kindly granted permission to reprint his short article "Freedom to Think". Also, other present or former employees of various government departments, as well as organizations such as the National Archives and the Canada Institute for Scientific and Technical Information, in the regular course of their duties, assisted me in obtaining information. In addition, assistance of the staff of the Ottawa Public Library, the Library of Parliament and the library of the National Office of the Royal Astronomical Society of Canada is acknowledged.

Special acknowledgement is due to Commander (Ret'd) G. G. Croswell and Mrs. Wilbert B. Smith, both of whom provided valuable assistance and advice. Last but not least, the continuing patience, understanding, encouragement and secretarial assistance of my wife, Dorothy, cannot go without special thanks.

PREFACE

This book is not only about Unidentified Flying Objects (UFOs). It is also concerned with our way of life on Planet Earth and the manner in which it has stifled the solving of what the late Dr. James E. McDonald referred to as "the greatest scientific problem of our times". McDonald was Professor of Atmospheric Physics at the University of Arizona.

It represents twelve years of research beyond the twenty years which went into my first book, **Science, the Public and the UFO** (1967). I want to stress, however, that it does not represent all my research over the past twelve years. It does include most of what I have factually documented. Certain other matters regarding UFOs have had to be omitted because of a lack of complete documentation at this time. Perhaps they will form part of a subsequent book if full documentation is eventually obtained.

A major problem in the study of UFOs (Ufology) is the lack of time available to serious researchers who are employed in some other line of work. It has to be very much a spare time activity. This is one reason why the UFO mystery has remained unsolved for so many years. Government and government-contracted studies have been inadequate for various reasons outlined in this book and although by far the great majority of research has been conducted by private individuals and groups, we are at it only on a part-time basis.

I wish to pay tribute to the many scientists and other scholars cited in this book, living and dead, whose work in unorthodox areas of science has resulted in great breakthroughs in the understanding of our universe. Most, if not all of them, have suffered ridicule from their peers for working outside the accepted structure of science. They displayed great courage in doing so. In most cases, their discoveries are still not accepted by the Scientific Establishment. Yet, their work is in the record and History will one day give them their due.

THE UFO CONNECTION

TABLE OF CONTENTS

PART 1

A SCENARIO OF THE FUTURE

CHAPTER 1

POPULATION: ZERO

Down from the vast reaches of far-off space, from uncounted planets of solar systems seen only as a blur in the largest telescopes, and from nearby orbs familiar to us, descends a vast armada of ships and beings, to centre their attention upon Planet Earth. They have come from within the Milky Way galaxy in response to a cry of warning from orbiting space stations that an unbelievable holocaust was engulfing the entire Earth, girdling the equator, and stretching from pole to pole.

What had been a verdant and productive world at one time, with land, water and air in abundance for all, was now a blackened, arid and desolated globe with all life obliterated. The only report which these visitants could flash back to their bases was— "reached Earth too late; population: zero".

Orbit Base Centaur, high in a stationary orbit, five thousand miles over Banks Island in the Canadian arctic, had been the first of the alien observation posts to raise the alarm throughout the nearby area of the galaxy. The electronic scanners had detected the launching of the missile attack at the precise moment they were fired from the orbiting satellites. Centaur's signals flashed to all space patrols in Galaxy Section M2, calling them in for rescue operations on Planet Earth.

Only seconds later, the retaliatory missile launch was detected on the opposite side of the planet and the anti-missile missiles were speeding towards their targets almost immediately. Earth technology had reached the stage where detection, tracking and guidance systems of missiles were so highly sensitive and accurate that every anti-missile missile could invariably seek out and destroy its target missile. There could be only one result. All of the hundreds of missiles launched in the attack were intercepted just over half way to their targets, high over the barren arctic regions. Instead of many hydrogen explosions occurring over a wide area on opposite sides of the globe, hundreds of double hydrogen explosions (missile exploding missile) all occurred in a small area within seconds of each other.

The nuclear chain reaction was predictable, but smug Earthman had as usual chosen to ignore the inevitable. The fireball which spread with electrifying speed around the entire planet and reached down to the surface in four seconds, eventually was visible from Alpha Centauri, four and one-half light-years distant.

There being nothing the space rescue teams could do, as everything on the face of the Earth was utterly destroyed by vaporization, including every drop of water in the oceans, they withdrew from their vantage point in space and returned to their various bases. Orbiting bases were left in position to monitor the surface condition of the Earth so the space people would know when it was safe to return to retrieve the historical records Earthmen had carefully buried deep underground over the years. It was as though Earthman had always subconsciously known the destiny of his planet and wanted to ensure that someday other races on other worlds would read his history and know that Earthman lived, and died, here. Little did he know that other, superior races already knew everything about him as they had been visiting Earth for many thousands of years, sometimes secretly, but often openly. Whenever one generation accepted the fact that visitors from space had appeared on Earth, the next generation simply rejected the whole thing and classed the reports of their forebears as myths and fairy tales. Whenever sound evidence of such visitations was unearthed years later, some other way of "explaining" the evidence was always found. Earthman was expert at that technique. If he did not wish to accept the truth of anything, he could always explain his observations in some other "more acceptable" way. Thus the folklore and mythology was believed to be fiction, and man was too blinded by his own conceit to see it as truth.

After several years, the violent, churning, superheated mass of gas now comprising the Earth's atmosphere cooled and released its cargo of black radioactive soot on the already black soil. It fell like snow over the entire face of the globe, and continued to pour down for weeks, until the whole planet was buried to a depth of several feet. This was the shroud covering the blackened corpse of a once-lively planet.

When the fall finally and slowly came to an end, and the violent winds had quietened, there remained an atmosphere of smoke and deadly radioactive gases as a cover to hide the blackened Earth from the eyes of passing space travellers. The Earth had returned to a state very similar to what had been hundreds of millions of years previously, surrounded by hot, poisonous gas incapable of supporting any form of life.

It was now possible, however, for a properly equipped expedition from other solar systems in the galaxy to land on Earth for the purpose of retrieving the buried records of the destroyed population. As the underground locations of these were already known as a result of the constant surveillance to which the planet had been subjected by manned spacecraft, it was not a difficult task to effect the retrieval. The Atlantic Rift, that great mountain chain splitting the Atlantic Ocean (now devoid of water) was used as the basis for determination of longitude by the expedition. Wearing radiation-proof space suits, the expedition members sank shafts into the Earth with laser drills and the sealed cannisters were withdrawn from their resting places by means of magnetic force. The entire operation lasted no more than twenty minutes.

The historical records recovered had represented, to Earthmen, a factual record of man on Earth. How little he realized how misled he was! Records of the same events were written by different people in different countries, and they seldom agreed. Even men of differing political bent wrote opposing versions. The inhabitants of each country believed in the accuracy of their own records, but they couldn't all be correct. In many cases, none were. Also, the records were often so incomplete that false interpretations were made as to the actual events which occurred. This was particularly so in the case of archeological findings. Man constantly interpreted his findings in terms of what he wanted to believe, and in ways of "fitting the pattern" he had devised. He never learned to accept his findings for what they were regardless of his preconceived ideas. There were the few exceptions, of course, who could accept facts for what they were, and tried to correct Earthman's view of his own history, but these were scoffed at and rejected by the Establishment. The fact that many races of Man had lived on Earth and had built advanced technological civilizations tens of thousands of years before even the earliest known records, of about 4000 B.C., was just not acceptable, despite the evidence pointing directly to this fact. This didn't fit the pattern. Man's constant habit of fragmenting knowledge into specialized fields always prevented him from seeing the true situation. Many signs were always before him to show him the truth but he would not see. Instead of questioning the accepted pattern of his surroundings when facts were observed which "didn't fit" the Establishment would reject the facts. This was why it took until the beginning of the 19th century for science to accept the fact that meteorites fall from the sky. They didn't fit the concept of man's surroundings at that time, and therefore "stones couldn't fall from the sky". Nevertheless, they fell. And in a similar way, the Establishment could not accept the fact that their planet was under constant surveillance by races of men more highly evolved than they. This didn't fit the pattern either, so despite the fact of hundreds of thousands of sightings of Unidentified Flying Objects, they always had to be explained in terms of something which fitted the neat little pattern, whether the explanations matched the facts or not.

And so Man blundered on, content with the great advances he thought he was making in understanding himself and his surroundings.

The historical records make it clear that one of the major reasons why Earthman could not accept the existence of intelligent life throughout the universe, and the ability of such beings to travel between solar systems, and even between galaxies, was his acceptance of scientific teachings, many of which were founded on false premises. He thought he understood the nature and structure of the universe fairly well. According to the picture of the universe as understood by Earthman, interstellar travel was simply impossible, therefore the matter was closed. His false understanding of the conditions on other planets within his own solar system blinded him to the existence of life even that close to home.

Earthman, due to a constant desire for recognition by his fellows, always took the shortest route by specializing in a particular area of knowledge, and ignoring all others. Thus, he was never able to see the whole picture and could not see that there had to be a Creator who designed the entire, marvellous and awe-inspiring universe for a purpose, and that this purpose was for the existence of life throughout its entirety. His mind was not open to facts which did not fit the picture he already held in his

4

mind. If a fact didn't fit, it was ignored. Revolutionary theories were considered the products of lunatics. Had Earthman not been so blind, he would have recognized that a new theory of the structure and nature of the universe was much more likely to describe the universe as it really is, than the image he had of a physical universe. He was fooled by illusions. He misinterpreted what he saw. He took the wrong road and thus missed the beautiful and glorious truth.

CHAPTER 2

A HISTORY LESSON

"Why is it," asked Jon, his blue eyes curious and sparkling, "that Earthlings consistently had so much trouble on their world?" While Ashura, his teacher, pondered this question, Jon lowered his husky five feet eleven frame into an easy chair and crossed his hands over his form fitting silver coverall.

After a lengthy pause, obviously having given deep and thoughtful reflection to the form of his reply, Ashura began. "Our friends on Planet Earth were obsessed with personal power, greed and lack of consideration for others. Empire-building, in both a personal and political sense, was a major contribution to their downfall. Any empire they built caused detrimental effects to others. The benefits for mankind as a whole were not considered. Personal fortunes were made through suppression of other people despite the fact the financiers could boast of the vast employment their enterprises provided for others.

"Political empires were founded through bloodshed. Throughout history, nations conquered and subdued other nations out of sheer greed for territory and its natural resources without regard for the people already living there. One of the best examples was the conquering of the Americas by the white man. To the day of Earth's destruction, hundreds of years after the subjection of the "Indian" peoples, the "Indians" remained a subject race in what was once their own land. Despite all the boasting of Europeans about how they brought civilization to the American continent and opened up its vast resources for the use of the world, the fact remains that this was accomplished only after terrible bloodshed and the permanent subjection of a race of fellow human beings. The same benefits could have been achieved by other means without loss of life and the "Indian" peoples would have remained a proud, progressive and prosperous race, enjoying the benefits of a technologically advanced society side by side with their white brethren.

"In the southern portion of the great continent called Africa" he continued, pointing it out on a large globe of Earth, "a handful of outsiders from Europe usurped power from the natives, acquired their land, and treated them in a cruel, unjust barbaric manner. The seeds of self-destruction were again being sown.

"Some Earthlings were even so naive as to believe that a large-scale·war every so often assisted in controlling population growth. Shortsightedness was a failing inherent in Earthman. Wars never succeeded in controlling population growth as history well proves. Any population decrease during a war was always more than compensated for shortly after the war ended.

"Throughout the planet, through all ages, some men achieved great power and tremendous wealth by suppression of others and limiting their freedom, to prevent anyone else from rising to power and wealth and thus be in a position to challenge their authority and position."

After a thoughtful pause, Ashura then continued. "Another form of shortsightedness—narrowmindedness—was embedded in their religious thinking. Earthlings had a profusion of religions, all varying in degree of detail but nearly all professing belief in the same Supreme Being, the Creator, despite the different names by which He was known. Few people ever recognized that the simple bases of all their religions were common to all. In addition to the same God, another common factor was the Golden Rule which we abide by.

"The Golden Rule is so simple to follow" said Ashura, "as you well know, Jon. Adhering to it in all activities would have brought peace, contentment and prosperity for all on Earth. No rule for social behaviour was ever more frequently disregarded than this. More wars were fought and more mortal lives snuffed out as a direct result of religious differences than from any other single cause.

"Yet the differences were only ones of detail. While professing to follow the teaching of the Creator they slaughtered each other at every opportunity, completely contrary to Supreme teachings. All the while, they would offer prayers asking for Supreme blessing in progressing their carnage, each side in a battle believing that they alone had God on their side and that He would help them carry out their bloodshed of His own children. Earthlings had the conceit to consider themselves civilized yet would consistently slaughter their fellow man for no other reason than that their brothers followed a somewhat different religion. Then they would go to their temples or churches and piously delude themselves into believing they were religious people, and that those who did not attend were pagans. They would deck themselves out like peacocks to impress their neighbours in church and look down their noses at any poor soul who could not afford to deck himself out similarly, considering him a disgrace to the church for not wearing finer clothing to Sunday worship.

"Yes, my son, the people of Earth were a strange lot. Filled with what they thought was their own importance, they neglected the importance of their fellow man. This was their downfall. Even sadder, they never learned by their mistakes. The human race on Planet Earth was almost wiped out on several occasions and always through the same cause. Earthmen were so filled with conceit they would never recognize the evidence before their eyes which proved the existence and total destruction of vast civilizations in previous ages. Their "learned men" always moulded any facts discovered to fit into their blind belief that their civilization of a mere few thousand years was the only one to have existed. Facts which came to light, contrary to this ingrained belief, were disregarded, suppressed, destroyed or deliberately lied about to make them "fit in" with the general belief. When individuals would discover some of those facts and bring them to light, the "experts" made them appear as fools in the eyes of the world. There is no easier way to close a man's mouth than for a man with a closed mind to make him appear the fool before his fellows. The people lived continually under an inquisitional regime where the weapon most frequently employed against non-conformist reality was derision.

"When it came to global thinking, they proved themselves totally inadequate", Ashura continued. "They organized a world body called the United Nations Organization which admittedly performed many useful services for underdeveloped nations. It did not keep peace in the world, despite many "peace-keeping forces" deployed around the planet between potential battle-lines. When any nation was intent upon waging war, it simply ignored the United Nations and its "peace-keepers". This was common with the members of the United Nations—family members destroying each other. The U.N. as a group was powerless to prevent this.

"Earthlings talked in terms of Martians, Venusians and Moon-men when speculating on the existence of intelligent life outside their own planet. They talked of possible visits to Earth by

9

extraterrestrial beings. But when they sent their own spacecraft to their moon, and to the planets Mars and Venus of their own solar system, they implanted a national flag of their countries United States of America and Russia. They were not thinking in global terms. Had they done so, they would have planted a flag of Planet Earth.

"Until they discovered the means of rapid communications including transportation, national or political boundaries were necessary for the administration of the affairs of a group of people due to the time required to accomplish anything over great distances.

"As their technology advanced, to include high speed air travel and world-wide telephone, radio, television and computer networks, the need for political barriers rapidly declined. All peoples of the Earth became as next door neighbours in the sense that the distances separating them—and hence the lack of knowledge of what each was doing—disappeared. Their communications technology was approaching our own. At the flick of a switch, or the press of a button, they could see their fellow men on the opposite side of the planet starving to death in squalor, and watch scenes of battle as they actually occurred. They could see and talk to their spacecraft crews inside their ships as they traversed space, just as we do. Through the marvels of rapid communication they were able to acquire far more knowledge of their own world in a very short time than previous generations had been able to acquire in a lifetime. Yet they still did not think of their world as one community.

"Although they had great pride in their science and technology, they did not have it under control. You see, my son, technology must be the servant of man, not his master. If technology is capable at times of doing things against the desires or command of man, it is not under full control, which means that technology, and not man, is master. Two examples will suffice to make clear how man failed in this respect. One was concerned with the electric power distribution system in their continent of North America, as you can see here on this globe. During the decade of the 1960s by their time reckoning, a number of failures occurred in this vast distribution system causing black-outs over large areas. The most serious one occurred in their year 1965 when a vast area involving tens of millions of people was affected. Although the points of technical failure were quickly located and corrective action taken, they never did discover the underlying causes of these failures, only the points of failure. They never did come to understand that we ourselves caused these power failures in an attempt to open their eyes to their lack of mastery of their own technology.":

"I see what you mean", said Jon. "What was the other example?" Ashura stood up and walked to a window, then continued. "It was the effects of radiation on children in the Utah part of North America after test explosions of hydrogen bombs in the early part of the decade of their 1950s. Their officials were convinced that no harm could result from these nuclear tests, they were so certain of their knowledge and expertise. Yet the isotope iodine 131 escaped, drifted to Utah farms, was foraged by cows, passed to children in their milk and was gathered in high concentration in their thyroid glands. Here, in a period of a few weeks, the iodine 131 released its radiation.

"Earthlings were adept at forging ahead with technological and biological "advances" without the slightest idea of their long term effects. Their consuming desire for power and superiority,economically, politically, militarily and so on, caused them to embark upon dangerous courses, blind to the consequences of their actions. Nuclear fallout, the widespread use of chemical detergents and insecticides, the use of harmful ingredients in medicinal drugs (such as thalidomide), the burning of petroleum fuels in internal combustion engines, and so on, are some examples of the way Earthlings blundered on their way, destroying their environment along with themselves.

"You know, my boy, Earth people were a strange lot in so many ways. They measured success in terms of money alone. Material wealth was all-important. Spiritual wealth meant little unless material wealth went with it. So you see, in the end only material wealth had any meaning to them.

"People who had not made any particular success of themselves, had few spiritual assets, and no more of the material type, could inherit or win a fortune and would immediately acquire status over others solely by their possession of money. They were exactly the same people in terms of achievement but the mere possession of money, even simply by chance, enabled them to acquire all the trappings and status symbols which made them **appear** to be highly successful and capable individuals. After acquiring their fortunes, they were no better in any way than

11

before but others would "bow and scrape" to them nevertheless.

"Even in situations where a man, through his ability, honesty and diligence, was able to amass a fortune quickly and changed his style of living accordingly, his family would all think that suddenly they were better than others "because they were rich" even though they contributed in no way to the success of the family head. Did the father's success suddenly transform them into "better people"? "Certainly not" answered Jon. "They were no better than before."

"A man with money was always assumed to know more than one who had none", Ashura went on. "Money was invariably equated with intelligence. It was always the rich man whose opinions were sought whether he acquired his wealth by virtue of superior intelligence or not.

"Another way in which Earthman's lack of control of his own way of life was very evident was in the number of hospitals they found necessary. Hospitals, too, were a status symbol. The thinking was that the larger and the better equipped, and the more hospitals they had in any community, was an indication of greater community success. It was an outward symbol to which city government officials could proudly point to visitors, of how well they were caring for the sick and injured.

What they never seemed to realize was that the need for more and more hospital beds was in reality a measure of how badly people were living. Most of the illness and injury they experienced was the direct result of their lifestyle. The food they ate, the way they prepared it, the additives put in for colouring and flavour, the polluted air they breathed and polluted water they drank, were major contributors to illness and disease. The thoughtless manner in which they worked and played resulted in a tremendous toll of injuries. No wonder they needed so many hospitals. Had they changed their way of living, they would have been able to boast about how few hospital beds were really needed. This would have been a worthy measure of their success in living."

"What was the meaning of the term 'peaceful co-existence'?" Jon inquired. "I have seen references to this term in the records of Earth from its latter years."

"This meant that each nation or race could go its own way yet keep peace with other nations" replied Ashura, after pondering this one for a moment. "The term implied differences between people (race, religion, etc.) and accepted these differences. But in truth there were no real differences—only imaginary ones. Efforts should have been directed towards eliminating such imaginary barriers and living as a world community—as one great family—not as 'co-existing.'

"Differences in religions create barriers. If all the commonality among religions had been retained and the many differences of detail discarded, a big step forward would have resulted.

"There was no reason why the entire Planet Earth should not have enjoyed a high standard of living with peace, contentment and good health for all. There was no reason why the average suburban-type North American home could not have been available to all throughout the Planet. In many cases, populations were too great, the result of lack of education, and suppression by the churches. **Opportunity** was what most people lacked. They should have been provided the opportunity to improve themselves. All races were equal—some just didn't have the opportunity available to others.

"Technology made many things available to improve the standard of living of certain groups of people, to reduce drudgery, increase recreation time, etc., but they were only available to those who could afford them. The poor areas of the world lacked those conveniences because they couldn't afford them. Not nearly enough effort was ever made in directing efforts towards making it possible for poor people to improve themselves.

"Tremendous technological advances were made in their twentieth century, but Earthman did not progress morally, socially or spiritually. He, in fact, was going down hill all the time while, in his ignorance, he thought he was advancing.

"Yes, my son" said Ashura, slipping back into his chair, "the people of Earth were blind to truth. This blindness brought about their own destruction. Not seeing simple truth for what it was, no other end was possible. The inevitable occurred and we foresaw it long ago. You see, only good can come from truth and had Earthman seen it, the Earth race could only have progressed continually upward. And so another chapter in the long history of Planet Earth has ended in destruction. One day far in the future we will again seed the planet and a new race will once again make an attempt to reach the stars."

13

PART 2

MEANWHILE . . .

CHAPTER 3

SO YOU THINK THE FLYING SAUCER ISSUE IS DEAD?

The mystery of Unidentified Flying Objects (UFOs) or Flying Saucers has been the source of controversy for thirty years. For many people, it all began in 1947 when Kenneth Arnold, a private pilot in the U.S.A., reported a formation of nine silver discs over Mount Rainier in the state of Washington. Since then, millions of people around the world in all walks of life, young and old, have reported seeing strange aerial objects which could not be identified. A Gallup Poll in 1978 disclosed that over ten per cent of adult Canadians had seen what they believed to be UFOs. In addition, of those aware of UFOs, forty-six per cent believe they are real and not just a figment of someone's imagination.[1] A quite similar situation exists in the U.S. where a Gallup Poll was also conducted. Of the 15,000,000 Americans who have seen what they believed to be UFOs, few reported them to the U.S. Air Force, the official American investigating agency until 1969. The Air Force files contain only 13,134 reports.[2]

Another significant finding in the U.S. Gallup Poll, conducted in November 1973, was that the greater the education, the more likely that an individual believes in UFOs.[3] This contradicts those who believe that only uneducated people have such a belief.

A similar situation exists around the world. Most people refrain from reporting their sightings for fear of ridicule, the weapon employed by governments and the scientific establishment to discourage sighting reports.

Of those sighting reports submitted to investigating bodies, about ten per cent remain unidentified after thorough study by experienced and capable investigators. This ten per cent constitutes the true UFOs. These are the hard core which cannot be explained in terms of known natural phenomena or man-made objects. It is only these which are of permanent interest and concern to UFO investigators. Once a sighting has been clearly identified as some known natural phenomenon or man-made object, it is no longer a UFO but an IFO (Identified Flying Object). An interesting fact is that the unidentified cases (after investigation) are not those with the least data to aid in explaining them, but those which have the most, and therefore present a true enigma.

Dr. J. Allen Hynek[4] has classified UFO reports into specific categories, as follows:[5]

NL	– Nocturnal Lights:	distant anomalous lights seen in the night sky.
DD	– Daylight Discs:	distant disc-like objects seen during the day.
RV	– Radar-Visual:	UFOs seen by radar and vision simultaneously.
CE I	– Close Encounter of the First Kind:	UFOs seen within 500 ft.
CE II	– Close Encounter of the Second Kind:	CEIs that leave behind physical traces.
CEIII	– Close Encounter of the Third Kind:	CEIs with humanoid occupants seen.

The Aerial Phenomena Research Organization of Tucson, Arizona, has added an additional category, (CEIV—Close Encounters of the Fourth Kind) which is reports of witnesses being abducted by UFO occupants.

Note that this classification system breaks down UFOs (ie., **un**identified objects) into various categories. I will go back one step and classify all sightings **reported by the observer.** We must keep in mind that of all sightings initially reported, only about ten per cent turn out, after thorough investigation, to be UFOs. That is, of all so-called UFOs reported by observers, about ninety per cent can be identified by competent investigators as known natural phenomena or man-made objects. My classification, therefore, of sighting reports of flying objects which the **observer** cannot identify, is:

> Class I — The sighting can be identified by a competent **investigator** as a known natural phenomenon or man-made object. This then represents an Identified Flying Object (IFO), and must be ignored. This class can also include hoaxes.

16

Class II — Sufficient data is available for a competent investigator to work with, but no explanation fits all the facts. The sighting thus represents an Unidentified Flying Object (UFO).

Class III — There is insufficient data for a competent investigator to classify the sighting as either Class I or Class II (IFO or UFO). These sightings must also be ignored, unless further evidence is later brought to light.

It is obvious that Dr. Hynek's classification of UFOs applies only to Class II sighting reports (see table below).

CLASSIFICATION OF SIGHTING REPORTS
Class I — IFO

Class II — UFO - nocturnal lights
       - daylight discs
       - radar/visual
       - CE I
       - CE II
       - CE III
       - CE IV

Class III — insufficient Data for classes I or II.

The importance of Class III reports should not be overlooked as an investigator must have enough facts to work with in order to classify a sighting as Class I or Class II. Lacking sufficient data for either classification, he must recognize Class III. Simply because the investigator cannot slot a report into Class I does not automatically make it a Class II sighting report. He must have enough data to justify saying it cannot be identified.

Various scientific (and unscientific) studies have been carried out over the years since 1947 in efforts to determine just what could explain the "unknowns". Many people have seriously suggested that hallucinations and hoaxes as well as over-imbibing produce the answer. Studies have shown, however, that such is not the case. One interesting study by Dr. David Saunders of 7025 cases in a computer file has shown that more sightings occur on Tuesday and Wednesday than on any other day of the week. The fewest occur on weekends.[6] This destroys the over-imbibing theory which we all know is more prevalent on weekends. Such explanations do account for some sightings, after investigation, and constitute a portion of the ninety per cent identified. The ten per cent still remains, and this percentage includes reports by people whose character, employment, social responsibilities and all other aspects of their day to day reliability have been checked and verified. Many are people whose livelihood depends entirely upon what they see and report (for example aircraft controllers, pilots, police officers, astronomers) who are not going to risk their jobs and reputations over faked flying saucers.

Those astronomers, mathematicians and physicists who have studied the subject extensively consider unconventional explanations (unknown natural phenomena, alien devices or specifiable or unspecifiable other causes) are more likely than hoaxes. This was found out in a survey of a group of North American scientists conducted by Dr. Peter Sturrock of Stanford University through questionnaires sent out to all members of the American Astronomical Society (professional astronomers, physicists and mathematicians). This survey also established that 62 members of the 1356 who returned the questionnaire had "witnessed or obtained an instrumental record of an event which they could not identify and which they thought may be related to the UFO phenomenon".[7] This clearly establishes that some scientists do indeed see UFOs. The same study further established that opinions correlate strongly with the time spent reading about the subject and that those scientists who have studied the subject are more willing to help in UFO research and are more likely to see a way to help.

The hard core of cases includes the multiple-witness type where two or more witnesses independent of each other reported the same thing. It also includes cases verified by radar at the same time as there were independant visual sightings, thus ruling out radar "ghosts". Some radar cases have even been verified by airborne electronic countermeasures equipment. Photographic evidence supports many sightings and even American Astronauts have seen and photographed UFOs in space.[8] To add to all this are the many cases of landings where burned marks have been left on the ground, tree branches have been broken and vegetation refuses to grow for years after. Thousands of people have experienced complete failure of automobile electrical systems during a close approach of a UFO. Many of these people were police officers on duty. The U.S. Air Force even admits to firing on UFOs during aerial chases by jet interceptors while at the same time claiming that UFOs don't exist.[9]

Hundreds of landing cases with reported contacts with occupants have occurred and such cases are classified as Close Encounters of the Third Kind (CE III). The most widely known case is that of Barney and Betty Hill, which occurred in 1961. This case invariably comes up in my formal talks and informal discussions. A high percentage of people have either read the book,[10] read a condensation in their local paper, or saw the TV movie about it. The impact this case has had on people is amazing.

Briefly the story is this. On the night of September 19, 1961, Barney and Betty Hill of Portsmouth, New Hampshire, were driving home from a visit in Canada, having crossed back into the U.S.A. south of Montreal. It was a bright clear night with an almost full moon. The stars were brilliant as they drove through the New Hampshire mountains along U.S. 3, expecting to be home in Portsmouth by 2:30 next morning, or 3:00 at the very latest.

At close to 11:00 p.m. the Hills spotted what appeared to be a moving star but after close observation for some time its erratic movements convinced them it could not be a star. Their curiosity aroused, they continued along the deserted winding highway and even stopped to watch the moving light through binoculars. They suspected it was a plane and they noted a blinking series of lights which rotated around the sides of the object, which began to follow them. As the object got closer Barney got out of the car for a better look from a nearby field. It was obvious that it was huge and apparently had a row of windows and Barney could see a number of humanoid beings watching him. He became terrified as the object was making an approach to land, and ran back to the car and they drove off. Shortly, he and Betty heard a beep-beep-beep which they could not identify and they became drowsy. Later, they heard this beeping again and the drowsiness wore off, as they were continuing along the highway. They then discovered that there was about two hours which they could not account for and the sighting of the UFO bothered them.

The Hills were troubled by unexplained dreams and anxiety about the missing two hours and after about two years visited a Boston psychiatrist. After several months of weekly hypnosis sessions, the bizarre events of that night in 1961 were revealed.

Under hypnosis, both Betty and Barney separately told of

19

being taken aboard a spacecraft by the occupants. Neither one was made aware of what the other had revealed until some time later. Both their stories agreed in considerable detail. They revealed that they had been taken aboard this craft, were medically examined, and then released after having been given the hypnotic suggestion that they would remember nothing of the experience.

Betty also told, under hypnosis, how she asked the strange beings where they came from and she was shown a star chart which supposedly included their home base. Betty drew this chart under post-hypnotic suggestion and it was subsequently published.[11] An Ohio school teacher, amateur astronomer and member of Mensa , Marjorie Fish, wondered if the objects shown on the chart might represent some actual pattern of celestial objects. Fish reasoned that if the stars in the Hill map corresponded to a pattern of real stars it might be possible to pinpoint the origin of the space travellers. She then constructed several three-dimensional models of the solar neighbourhood in hopes of detecting the pattern in the Hill map. Using beads dangling on threads, she recreated our stellar environment from data in the current official star catalogues. Eventually, after a number of models were built, she was able to detect a pattern very closely resembling that drawn by Betty. This pattern could only be detected while viewing our solar system from the angle of that particular cluster of stars. That is, it was the view as would be seen by an observer "out there", not that of an observer on Earth.[12]

It turned out that three stars in Marjorie Fish's model did not quite match Betty Hill's chart. But then, a little while later, a new star catalogue was issued which gave the newest data on star positions. Marjorie had to adjust the positions of these beads to conform to the latest data available on the distances of the stars concerned. Now, on rechecking the pattern visually, it matched with Betty's chart! So we have a situation whereby Betty Hill drew a star chart in 1963 which contained the correct positions of certain stars—information not possessed by any astronomer at that time, as the correct positions were not discovered until several years later.

This could mean only one thing—that Betty Hill received her information from the source she claimed she did—that her story was true.

A large unidentified, lighted object over sixty feet in diameter descended from the sky in front of RCMP witnesses, settled onto the sea, then slowly sank beneath the waves. Navy divers failed to find a trace of it on the bottom. Did it or did it not exist? If so, what was it?

This incident occurred on the night of October 4th, 1967 off the coast of Shag Harbour, Nova Scotia. A number of boats,including a Coast Guard vessel with RCMP officers aboard rushed to the scene of the landing. Observers aboard the vessels reported a thick yellow foam on the surface at the apparent point of impact.

The Royal Canadian Navy sent a team of seven divers to search the sea bottom but gave up after four days, having found nothing. Civil and military authorities confirmed no aircraft was missing.[13]

Docs finding nothing there prove there was nothing there to start with? We have RCMP officers as witnesses to the fact that a large, lighted flying object landed on the sea and sank. This incident clearly shows that UFOs are elusive, not illusions.

At about 5 a.m. on New Year's morning, 1970, at the Cowichan District Hospital in Duncan, B.C., Miss Doreen Kendall, a practical nurse, was checking on a patient and, deciding that the woman's restless sleep was due to being too warm, she decided to open a window. As she pulled open the drapes a brilliant light hit her in the eyes. It was still dark outside, but about 60 feet away, right above the children's ward there was an object so big and bright she could see it all clearly.

In Miss Kendall's words, "The object was circular, the bottom was silvery, like metal, and was shaped like a bowl. There was a string of bright lights around it like a necklace. The top was a dome made of something like glass. It was lit up from inside and I could see right into it."

She said there were two male-like figures in the craft. Their heads were encased in close-fitting dark material. The craft tilted and she was soon able to see to their knees. They were dressed in tight-fitting suits of the same material. Their hands were bare and had human-appearing flesh.

There was what appeared to be an instrument panel facing one of the occupants, with instruments of a variety of sizes.

When the occupants noticed Miss Kendall, the one at the instruments moved a lever and the object circled slowly in an anticlockwise direction.

At this point, Mrs. Frieda Wilson, R.N., joined Miss Kendall at the window, and saw the object circling and moving away. Then two other nurses, at another window, looked just in time to see the bright light moving off into the distance.[14]

This case represents a typical close encounter (CE III) where a clear and detailed description was possible, and humanoid figures were seen.

An employee of the Department of National Defence was driving with his wife and 15 year old son near the village of Hammond, Ontario, about 25 miles east of Ottawa, between 8 and 8:30 p.m. on April 22, 1969.

The weather was totally overcast with heavy rain. The man knew this area very well having lived there for some time. They spotted what they described as a huge drinking cup turned upside down, with two bright white lights and appeared to have a row of portholes with a pink light emanating from them. The object was about five feet above the ground and about 200 feet away, across an open field. The white lights lit up the whole field, as well as the interior of the car. The witness described a sound from the object as sounding like a generator.

The object then turned, zoomed over the trees at the edge of the field and then moved along over the nearby power line. The family watched the phenomenon for 15-20 minutes.[15]

Dr. Bruce McIntosh of National Research Council (NRC) thought this may have been a helicopter despite the witness's denial, as he was familiar with motors and helicopters. NRC checked out all sources of helicopters in the area and none were flying. Helicopters don't fly in such foul weather.

I am very familiar with day and night helicopter operations, and this was not a helicopter. Despite my vehement objections to this explanation, Dr. McIntosh insists that a helicopter is a "very plausible" explanation.[16]

I respect Dr. McIntosh as an astronomer but I consider myself more experienced and knowledgeable in helicopter operations than he is and I must continue to disagree with him.

This case is a good example of officialdom "explaining" a report whether or not the explanation is a logical or even a scientific one. Anything to settle the matter quickly.

Until May 20, 1967, Stephen Michalak of Winnipeg had no

interest in UFOs or other such phenomena. But on that day, Stephen, a 52 year old industrial mechanic went prospecting at Falcon Lake about 80 miles east of Winnipeg on the Trans Canada Highway and confronted a UFO on the ground. He is an amateur geologist and enjoys an opportunity to search out minerals.

Just after lunch his attention was attracted by the cackling of geese on the nearby swamp and his eyes then caught two scarlet lights in the clear sky above. They began to descend and assumed a definite cigar shape with a humped protrusion on each top. One object continued to descend to the ground 130 ft. away. Its companion hovered over the tree tops for a moment then suddenly sped up into the sky and disappeared.

Steve then watched the landed object change colour from brilliant scarlet to grey-red to grey to silver. "Exactly the same effect as hot metal when it cools down", he said. He was now able to discern more detail of what was apparently a disc-shaped craft. It was circular, about 35 ft. in diameter with sloping sides and a round dome-structure above the upper deck. Down the sloping side facing him were nine vent-like openings of about 6 × 9 inches. Each opening contained 30 small holes which, he thought, may have been ventilation or exhaust ports.

Michalak decided to sketch the machine and made several close approaches to observe in greater detail. He is also an amateur artist.

As the craft continued to cool he could feel waves of heat rolling from it, accompanied by a vile, nauseating odour like sulphur. As he approached again, he noticed a doorway appear in the side. From the opening came a brilliant violet light that lit up the ground despite the bright sunlight. Through the whistling of air and a continuous whine from the craft, Michalak heard the distinct sound of three voices.[17] He saw no occupants but heard only voices coming from inside. He attempted communication in several languages but was unsuccessful. He approached, lowered the green lenses of his safety goggles (which he wore to protect his eyes from rock chips) and looked inside. He was able to observe small lights flashing in random fashion throughout the interior. Upon stepping back, the doorway closed.

Completely astonished by these events, he again approached the craft and placed his glove-covered hand on the shiny side. His glove melted on contact. At that instant, the craft angled slightly upward and Michalak felt a burning sensation on his chest. His outer shirt caught fire and he tore it and his undershirt from his body. One of the vent-like openings on the side had emitted a blast of heat and he was sent reeling by the force. When he was able to look up again the craft was above the tree tops and within a minute was out of sight.

A tremendous odour of sulphur permeated the area and waves of nausea swept over Michalak. Gathering up his prospecting equipment he began an agonizing trek the two miles back to the highway. Wretchedly ill, he estimated he vomited over 200 times during his two-hour trek back. At the highway he attempted to flag down an RCMP patrol car which refused to stop.

To make a long story short, after having difficulty getting medical assistance, he returned to Winnipeg and was immediately admitted to hospital and began a long period of treatment for a mysterious malady that would plague him for a year and a half. He was treated for first degree burns and released. He suffered considerable weight loss. No abnormal radiation level was detected. After two weeks, a rash appeared on his chest. Every three to four months for the next year and a half his symptoms returned. In August, 1968 he was stricken with a geometric pattern of burns on his chest as well as nausea and blackouts. Twenty-seven doctors examined Michalak during this period and none was able to properly diagnose his illness.[18]

An investigation was conducted by the Departments of Health and Welfare and National Defence, the National Research Council, the University of Colorado, and the Canadian Aerial Phenomena Research Organization.

Radioactivity was detected at the site and it was suggested this originated with the dial of Michalak's watch! Pieces of metal, analyzed as being 92-96% silver were found on the landing site. Silver fragments indicated that the metal had been subjected to heat at the site.

The Department of National Defence was asked by the then Member of Parliament, Ed Schreyer, (now our Governor General) to make the investigation results public. Defence Minister Leo Cadieux refused.

Michalak's high medical bills including a two week visit to the Mayo Clinic in Rochester for treatment were financed from his own pocket.[19] If Michalak perpetrated a hoax, it was a costly venture.

Later, MP Barry Mather's persistence resulted in the Michalak file being tabled in the House of Commons. It was claimed that the file was complete except for deletion of some names and inter-office memos.[20] I was granted the privilege of viewing this file by Mr. Mather and I was thus able to make a general comparison with the file as I saw it originally at NRC. Let me assure you the file was quite incomplete, thus the House was misled. Even when I originally viewed it at NRC some papers were missing, e.g. RCMP reports which were referred to in other papers and some results of laboratory tests on articles submitted by Michalak for testing.[21] It is fair to withhold names of witnesses who wish to remain anonymous but in this case there was only one witness and he was already known. Why the secrecy?

This case serves as an excellent example of the government being very much involved in UFO investigation but throwing a cloud of secrecy over the results.

The case was an excellent close encounter of the second kind, with landing traces and physical effects.

Rick and Donna Bouchard of Ottawa, and their two children, were driving home at approximately 10:40 p.m. on the night of November 8, 1973, when they experienced something they will never forget.

They had been out to see their new house in Vars, about 15 miles east of Ottawa, and were travelling along a 10 mile stretch of a new four-lane divided highway being built to connect Ottawa with Montreal, 120 miles away. This stretch of road, because it was incomplete and served only a few small towns by connecting overpasses, was generally nearly deserted. The highway has been cut through bush and farmland and at night only the odd light from a farm house here and there can be seen. The median strip is exceptionally wide and over much of its length contains trees and heavy bush making viewing of cars in the opposite lanes difficult at most times.

The night was dark, the road deserted and Rick and his family were anxious to get back home. Having entered the new highway 417 at the Vars crossroad, they headed west towards Ottawa in their pick-up truck. About a mile and a half along the road, Rick, a ticket clerk with Canadian National Railways in Ottawa, spotted brilliant lights in his side mirror. (The view from his rear mirror was blocked by a tarpaulin.) At first he thought it was a truck which had suddenly caught up to him but quickly realized that as the road is so straight and deserted this couldn't have happened unless the truck had been travelling with lights off and suddenly turned them on immediately behind him. He also quickly realized that although the lights were brilliant, they were in fact a large number of small lights rotating quickly and apparently "bouncing up and down". His wife Donna spotted the lights about the same time in the right side mirror. Both were puzzled and frightened because the strange lights were so close they seemed to be "hanging on the rear bumper". The object was large enough to protrude a couple of feet on both sides of the truck. Rick pressed his foot down on the accelerator in an attempt to put more distance between his truck and his pursuer but the object stuck with them as their speed reached 97 mph on the speedometer.

After a short distance the object was seen to drop back and rise to tree-top level and then out of the field of the mirrors and immediately dived down to close in on them again to a distance of about 10 ft. By this time Rick yelled to Donna to grab the axe which was stowed under the seat as self-defence was uppermost in his mind at this point. The children were unable to see anything due to their position low on the seat between Rick and Donna but were terribly frightened because of their parents' fears.

Once more, the brightly lighted object, described as round, somewhat flat on the bottom and curved on top, fell back and climbed out of sight and again dived down after them. Rick estimates it must have flown at 300 mph during these dives as it caught up so rapidly and he was doing just under 100 mph himself.

There are five overpasses on this stretch of road which 417 passes under and Rick and Donna swear that the UFO flew under at least one of these (Anderson Road) "right on their tail".

Just after they passed under this overpass, the last one before the end of the highway, the UFO just "disappeared". But Rick was so frightened, he kept going at full speed, not knowing whether the object might dive after him again. At that time, when the median ended, the road curved in a wide arc to the right for about 90 degrees, where it met the Russell Road, with a stop sign at the intersection. Rick negotiated the curve at full speed, he claims, and although he has no way of explaining how he managed it, went through the stop sign and turned left 90° on to Russell Road to head into Ottawa. Donna was convinced they were going to end up in the field across Russell Road and likewise cannot explain the "miracle" of how the right angle turn was negotiated at that speed.

Rick himself was so amazed that the next day he went out there again in daylight and tried the same thing but found he couldn't even negotiate the wide curve without slowing to 60 mph, let alone make the right angle turn at the intersection. Yet both are certain his foot was still "on the floor" the previous evening as their speed was so fast. A subsequent trip at night made him realize that the "bouncing" of the lighted object was the result of his mirror vibrating. This became apparent when he watched an auto's lights behind him.

During the wild chase of 8.5 miles only two other cars were seen, both travelling in the opposite direction, across the wide median strip. Rick blasted his horn consistently in some sort of attempt to attract attention to his predicament but in any event there was little anyone else could do to help him. The occupants of neither car gave any indication of having seen the chase.

Upon nearing Cyrville on the edge of Ottawa, he spotted a police car of the Gloucester Police Department and reported the incident. The police confirmed to me the very shaken and excited state of the Bouchards. Two other police forces were also alerted and several cars were dispatched to the scene but nothing was seen. Also confirmed.

Rick drove to Montfort Hospital Emergency Ward for treatment of their nervous and upset condition. Their treatment here has been confirmed by the hospital, where the nurse on duty that night stated to me that the Bouchards were "very shaken up, very upset and very pale" and that they were given appropriate treatment before release.

The weather conditions were not conducive to any unusual conditions that night as a check with the weather office has confirmed—nothing to cause ball lightning, reflections, an inversion layer (there wasn't one) or any other unusual phenomena. The moon was between three-quarters and new, the sky mainly clear with a few scattered clouds.

As usual, attempts to explain it all away were made, and a news item pointed out that "highway 417 runs parallel to the approach path of an Uplands airport runway". The airport is several miles away and anyone with any knowledge of aircraft knows that this particular incident could not possibly have been an aircraft on its landing approach. It is worthy of note that the NRC, Canada's official UFO investigating agency, never contacted Rick or Donna.

The only aspect of this incident which, at date of writing, is incomplete is substantiation of the sighting by independent witnesses. Much effort has gone into an attempt to locate the occupants of the two autos travelling in the opposite direction. At one point, it appeared that one such witness had been found, but upon further checking, the witness concerned was clearly involved with a different case, in the same general area.

Should the occupants of one or both of these cars come forth to verify this incident, the fact that it did occur as claimed by the Bouchards, will be open to no doubt.

The experience of Rick and his family turns out to be just one of many incidents along this lonely stretch of dark highway on the outskirts of Ottawa. Rick's friend Ron Hamelin went out a few hours later, after hearing Rick's story, and claims to have seen a huge white light maintaining a distance of about 400 ft. behind him and taking up both lanes of the eastbound road, but did not threaten him in any way.

On December 1, 1973, Mrs. Nora Larocque of Lucerne, Quebec, and her 12 year old son were travelling eastwards on the same stretch and had an experience similar to that of Ron Hamelin. She stopped a couple of times to see if the object would overtake her, but it always stopped when she did. It was a huge white light with a small red light on top. Finally, the light just "disappeared".[22]

As well as these, a number of others have had frightening experiences with huge weird lights along this road and adjacent area during a short period of several weeks. Something, whatever it is, had a strange interest in this area. Thorough investigation, including in-depth interviews with the witnesses and detailed verification of all aspects of the witnesses' stories, fail to disclose any explanation to account for these incidents, including hoaxes, reflections, aircraft and other usual "explanations". Several months of investigation forced me to leave the Bouchards' experience, as well as the many others on the same stretch of road, in the "unidentified" category (Class II CE Is). Early in 1978, another series of encounters occurred on this same stretch of road.

In the words of Dr. Clifford Wilson, a noted Australian scholar and archeologist:

> The days of doubt have ended. The fact is—whether we like it or not—the UFOs are here. They have landed in the U.S.A. and Australia, in England and France, in Russia and Mexico, at both the North and South Poles . . . some with occupants and some without.[23]

Yes indeed, the flying saucer issue is very much alive.

CHAPTER 4

PASSENGER TRAIN IN THE SKY

From out of the western night sky appeared a long stream of brilliant reddish objects arranged in organized groups, lumbering along at a somewhat leisurely pace, leaving rumbling noises behind. Witnesses to this event were startled by its orderliness and precision of flight. It was described by some as "like a great passenger train in the sky".

It was at about 9:05 on the evening of Sunday, February 9, 1913 when the inhabitants of an extended portion of the United States and Canada witnessed this strange aerial display which is evidently without parallel. It was even witnessed well out into the Atlantic Ocean by people on islands and aboard ship.

The display began with the appearance in the northwestern sky of a fiery red body which quickly grew larger as it approached and which was then seen to be followed by a long tail. Some observers state that the body was single, some that it was composed of two distinct parts and others that there were three parts, all travelling together and each followed by a long tail.

Many people, at first thought, believed they were witnessing a huge sky rocket, as it resembled a rocket in its colour and in the streaming of the tail behind. But strangely enough, there was no sign of the object dropping to earth. Instead, it continued to move forward on a horizontal path, apparently very deliberately, and continued to the southeast where it simply disappeared in the distance.

Immediately thereafter, other bodies were seen approaching from the northwest, from the same point as the first one. Onward they moved, at the same deliberate pace, in twos or threes or fours. They too had tails streaming behind though not so long nor so bright as in the first case. They followed the same route, headed for the same point in the southeastern sky.

Succeeding bodies were smaller and smaller until the ones at the end appeared to be just red sparks, some of which seemed to be snuffed out before reaching their destination. Some witnesses claimed there was a large "star" without a tail near the middle of this procession, with a similar one in the rear.

31

Dr. C. A. Chant, a famous Canadian astronomer who conducted a thorough study of this event from the witnesses' reports, published a detailed report on it.[1] He states that to most observers, the outstanding feature of the phenomenon was the slow majestic motion of the bodies, and almost equally remarkable was the perfect formation which they retained. Many compared them to a fleet of airships, with lights on either side and forward and aft. Others likened them to great battleships attended by cruisers and destroyers. Still others thought they resembled a brilliantly lighted passenger train travelling in sections, and seen from a distance of several miles.

A distinct rumbling sound like distant thunder was heard in many places just as the bodies were vanishing, or shortly afterwards. In some cases, three such sounds were heard at short intervals. A number of people felt a shaking of the earth or of the house.

The number of bodies seen has never been agreed upon. Most estimates are from fifteen to twenty, but some vary from sixty to one hundred. Some people said there were thousands. Various explanations can be given for the great discrepancy between these estimates. Those giving the small numbers probably refer only to the chief bodies and as some people have better eyesight than others, where one would see a single body, others would see its different parts, according to Dr. Chant. Those who reported the large numbers undoubtedly included fragments of the larger bodies, Dr. Chant said. A Cecil Carley, a pupil at Trenton (Ontario) High School who watched the amazing procession through an opera glass said "There were about ten groups in all, and each group as seen through the opera glass consisted of from twenty to forty meteors".[2]

Dr. Chant estimated, from a study of the scores of reports received, that the entire display lasted about 3.3 minutes at any one point and states "This is an extraordinarily long time for such a phenomenon, but there is good evidence that it is not an exaggeration."[3]

In Chant's paper, he had traced the path of these "meteors" from Mortlach, Saskatchewan to Bermuda, a distance of 2437 miles and he considered this path "quite without parallel".

Another interesting aspect of this event is that "the meteors were travelling practically parallel to the surface of the earth . . . the downward tendency, **if it existed**, was very slight."[4] (author's emphasis)

The height of the bodies was established by Chant at about 26 miles, but this figure was uncertain due to the wide variation in the calculations of sightings by different observers.[5] He later revised his figure to 34 miles.[6]

In calculating the probable speed of these bodies, Chant's lowest calculation was 5⅓ miles per second but he concluded that this was "probably too low" on the grounds that a body travelling close to the earth's surface as a satellite in space would travel at 5.0 miles per second. He goes on to state that as these bodies were moving in the atmosphere (as attested by their red colour) they could not have moved so slowly without being brought to earth. Ergo, as they were not brought to earth, their speed must have been somewhat higher than 5 mps.

Chant's highest estimate of speed was 9.5 miles per second and he ends with the safe conclusion that the speed (with respect to the earth's surface) was "greater than 5 and less than 10 miles per second".[7] He later narrowed this down to between 6 and 6.5 mps.[8]

These bodies must have maintained their speed throughout their visible journey of thousands of miles because they maintained their height. It has not been explained why the friction of the atmosphere did not slow them down enough to cause them to fall to earth after a short while. We are told by Chant that the entire distance covered took 4 to 5 minutes.[9] Is it conceivable that meteors travelling at such a low speed could maintain that speed and altitude within the atmosphere for such a tremendously long time?

As for the size of these bodies, estimating was very difficult, but Chant was inclined to think that the largest bodies were at least one hundred feet in diameter including the extensive envelope of heated air and smoke which surrounds a meteor in the atmosphere and becomes luminous throughout.[10]

W. F. Denning reports that the chances are good that these objects were closer to 38 miles high.[11] The atmosphere at such heights is much more rarefied and therefore it is more likely that meteors could maintain their altitude. The same gentleman reached the conclusion that their velocity was about 8 miles per second. He also remarked upon the fact that they maintained the same relative distances from each other throughout their journey. That is, they kept perfect formation in flight.

This event was indeed unusual and the strange aspects can be summarized as follows:

a.   no apparent descent towards the ground—the path was parallel, or almost parallel, to the earth's surface;

b.   in the streaming of the tails behind, as well as in the colour both of the head and the tail, they resembled rockets;

c.   perfect formation was retained throughout the display;

d.   the unprecedented length of the flight path (2437 miles minimum);

e.   the extraordinarily long time the display lasted (about 3.3 minutes);

f.   apparent movement as satellites of the Earth with the plane of the path "passing through the centre of the Earth and hence cutting its surface in a great circle";

g.   the slow speed of travel across the sky (20 to 30 seconds for each object) as seen from any one point;

h.   they were not intensely white as most meteors are (colour is related to speed);

i.   most of the "parts" which "broke off" apparently continued to follow the parent body continuously without loss of speed, and few were reported as appearing to fall to earth although some "sparks" appeared to die out.

j.   the time of 4 to 5 minutes for each object to cover its entire observed track.

Presumably any one meteor can be expected to have one or more unusual features, but the large number of unusual features in this case which were common to all or most of the objects would seem to indicate that the objects were the most extraordinary in recorded astronomical history.

This event was described by Chant as "quite without a parallel", "a very exceptional occurrence" and "truly extraordinary".

However, it turns out that this event was much more extraordinary than Chant realized when he prepared his report. O'Keefe reported in 1968 that subsequent to Chant's paper, many more reports of the same incident were brought to light which extended the track of the objects 300 miles further northwest to the Alberta/British Columbia border and 3300 miles further southeast to a point just below the equator off the coast of Brazil.[12]

So the objects are now known to have travelled over 6000 miles, maintaining speed and altitude, not just 2500 miles, which was considered "extraordinary". What word can be used to describe this 6000 mile flight of "meteors"? How about "impossible"?

Chant calculated that the objects travelled about 2500 miles in 4 to 5 minutes at a speed of more than 5.0 but less than 10.0 miles per second. If we divide 2500 by 4.5 we get 555 miles per minute and dividing again by 60 gives us 9.25 miles per second which fits within Chant's original limits.

Now, as the track or flight path actually covered over 6000 miles, let's find the elapsed time at a speed of 9.25 mps. Dividing 6000 by 9.25 we get 649 seconds, or 10 minutes 49 seconds.

What it now comes down to is that these objects, supposedly meteors, maintained their altitude and low speed despite atmospheric friction for almost 11 minutes!

Calculations were made by a British authority on meteors, M. Davidson in 1913, who insists the bodies must have had a speed near 4.93 mps, the velocity to cause a body to describe a circular orbit (ie, maintain its height) which these bodies evidently did. A greater velocity would imply an elliptic orbit and the bodies would rise from the surface of the earth, he says. Anything less, and the bodies would fall.[13]

Suppose, to keep it simple, we divide 6000 miles by 5 mps. We get 1200 seconds, which is 20 minutes. So depending on whose velocity we use the objects took anywhere from 10 to 20 minutes to cover their flight path!

It is understandable that Dr. Chant thought only in terms of meteors. In 1913 there was no other explanation available so they **had** to be meteors. However, in the light of what we now know about unknown objects in our skies, and about the extended flight path of these particular objects, the meteor explanation for this event must be challenged and re-examined. There is a large volume of data available on this event but no explanation fits all the facts. The report thus should be classed as a Class II sighting (UFO).

My view is supported by a well-known astronomer who holds a high position (who shall remain unnamed) who stated in writing to me:

> I, too have been puzzled by the "meteor" explanation and feel that, in the light of the full UFO phenomenon, this hypothesis must be seriously questioned.

CHAPTER 5

UFOs AT THE U.N.

In order to understand the present and to predict the future, we must understand the past. The study of the history of Ufology is as important as the history of any other subject if one is to grasp it.

To provide a complete and comprehensive history of Ufology would require several volumes. One excellent volume concerning its history in the U.S.A. has been written by Dr. David M. Jacobs.[1] A very small part of the Canadian history of the subject was included in my own earlier book, now out of print.[2]

In February 1969, I submitted a brief to the Special Senate Committee on Science Policy in an attempt to urge the government to take some positive action towards solving the UFO mystery. Needless to say, my brief was ignored apart from publishing it in the Proceedings of the Committee.[3] (See Annex 1).

If the distinct probability that we are under surveillance by alien beings does not require some sort of broad scientific policy then it only serves to show the fuzzy thinking on the part of the Senate Committee. On the other hand, can there be movements behind the scenes that the public is not privy to? I ask this question because although there is no action evident by the government, the Department of External Affairs has admitted serious concern over the UFO problem and states that several government departments maintain a close interest in the matter.[4]

One case in point has to be the Department of National Defence, although it steadfastly denies any current interest. The simple fact that UFOs (whatever they are) do exist, and are tracked on radar, are of necessity of interest to Air Defence Command despite the admission that they are not a threat to security. If the government does **not** know what UFOs are, then they could conceivably be Russian aerial devices used for surveillance purposes. This possibility alone has to be of concern to DND, otherwise why do we have an Air Defence Command (ADC) which is really part of NORAD? Does ADC calmly ignore all aerial objects which they cannot identify? This is really what DND is telling us. Frankly, I don't believe it.

As might have been predicted, the Canadian government has taken no action on this brief to the Special Senate Committee. None was recommended by the Committee. Besides this, the government is not prone to taking any positive and progressive steps in this field. Although my brief may have been read with interest, it was, in fact, ignored. No mention was made of UFO research in the subsequent Report of the Senate Committee and correspondence with Senator Lamontagne, the Chairman, elicited the information that the Committee was only interested in broad policies, not in specific programs.[5]

One of my recommendations in this brief was that Canada should establish the first fully-objective and open investigation, not clouded in a cloak of secrecy, and leaving no stones unturned. Our example to other nations should then provide the necessary encouragement for them to join us in this exciting quest so that eventually the United Nations Organization can be the global co-ordinator for the study. As it is clear that UFOs are a world-wide enigma, and their patterns of behaviour are also world-wide, the problem should be attacked on a global basis. The only suitable, and obvious, organization to attempt this, it would seem, is the U.N.

Several unsuccessful approaches have already been made. The first was by a Mr. Colman VonKeviczky, a former employee of the U.N. Secretariat, Office of Public Information, who was fired for his efforts in 1966. His firing was not, evidently, because of what he said, but because of the way he went about it. He issued a press release, unauthorized by the U.N. Later that year, he submitted a thick file on the subject to Secretary-General U Thant, who thanked him for his "voluntary efforts and interest in the matter".

VonKeviczky was informed in 1967 that the U.N. could not take any action on a submission from an individual, but only on submissions from Member States.

The next submission was a personally-presented brief to the U.N. Outer Space Affairs Group, by Dr. James E. McDonald, on June 7, 1967. In this brief, he urged the U.N. to "immediately undertake a review of the UFO problem". He also said that "the most probable hypothesis to account for the UFO phenomena is that these are some type of surveillance probes of extraterrestrial origin".[6]

Meanwhile, U Thant's personal interest in UFOs became widely known to Ufologists around the world. Knowing of this interest, I sent him a copy of my first book and received a kind acknowledgement.

In August 1970, U Thant visited Ottawa to open the International Congress of World Federalists. During this visit he was interviewed briefly by Mrs. I. V. Jacobi, a UFO reporter for an international organization. One of her questions was:

> Your Excellency, UFO researchers the world over know that you are kept well informed on the possibility that extraterrestrial spacecraft do visit our planet but these facts are classified to the world public. Is this correct?[7]

The same source reported that the Secretary-General nodded a hesitating yes and said "There are many things that I am forbidden to speak of". In response to a further question, he confirmed that the U.N. could investigate UFOs if one Member Nation would place the problem on the agenda.

In an attempt to verify U Thant's statements, I wrote to him in December that year seeking confirmation. In reply, I was informed by a staff member that as the Secretary-General's remarks were extemporaneous, no official text is available, but that U Thant does not believe he could have given the reply attributed to him. Did he, or did he not, make the statement? Was this an attempt to cover up a slip of the tongue? If he did make that statement it should not really surprise us as not even our Queen can make public statements which have not been written for her by the government.

On June 18th, 1966, Dr. J. Allen Hynek, mentioned in Chapter 3, and John Fuller, a respected journalist, were granted a one-hour interview with U Thant on the matter of UFOs and Thant expressed his strong interest in the subject. He also pointed out the similar concern that had been expressed to him by General Assembly members from several countries. He also stated that he was sympathetic to U.N. action and again stressed that such action would have to be initiated by a Member Nation.[8]

In March, 1971, I appealed to Prime Minister Trudeau to take the necessary steps to place the UFO problem on the agenda of the U.N. General Assembly. The reply from the Department of External Affairs stated:

The Canadian Government does not underestimate the serious-ness of the question of UFOs, and this matter is being kept under consideration and study in a number of departments and agencies.

Canada's representatives at the U.N. have maintained a close liaison with the Secretariat and other missions in New York on the subject, but do not consider that the prospects for the adoption of a resolution by the General Assembly at the present time are encouraging. If and when it appears that a resolution of the kind you mention would be likely to receive approval by the General Assembly, you may rest assured that the Canadian Government would be prepared to take all appropriate steps in this connection.[9]

On October 7th, 1976, Prime Minister Sir Eric Gairy of the Caribbean island Grenada addressed the General Assembly of the U.N. on the UFO issue. In this address, he stated:

One wonders why the existence of UFOs . . . continues to re-main a secret to those in whose archives repose useful information and other data. While we appreciate that some countries consider this to be in the interest of military expedience, I now urge that a different view be taken because it is my firm conviction that the world is ready, willing and ripe enough to accept these phenomena . . .[10]

The Prime Minister's comments and recommendations on unidentified flying objects and related research aroused very favourable world-wide reaction resulting in an invitation to him to attend the First International Congress on the UFO Phe-nomena held at Acapulco, Mexico from the 18th to 23rd April, 1977, organized by the Centre for Information and Investigation of UFO and Parapsychological Phenomena, and to deliver the feature address at the opening function. That Congress, at-tended by well-known and respected scientists and writers in the field, representatives of the major organizations of the world concerned with unidentified flying objects, unanimously passed a resolution acknowledging the great interest taken by the Prime Minister of Grenada in unidentified flying objects and related phenomena, supporting him in the courageous stand he took during two consecutive years (1975 and 1976) in bringing this matter to the attention of the General Assembly and urging him to continue in his effort for the establishment by the United Nations of an agency or a department for research into unidentified flying objects and related phenomena.

The Prime Minister of Grenada regarded his effort to intervene at the thirty-second session of the General Assembly as constituting the carrying out of a mandate emanating from the First International Congress and as expressing a new dynamic thrust to which his Government is deeply committed.

In an October 1977 address, Sir Eric was successful in having the matter of "UFOs and related phenomena" placed on the agenda of the 32nd General Assembly as item 123. The leader of the smallest nation in the western hemisphere easily succeeded in doing what Canada was reluctant to do.

Shortly thereafter, I was one of a group of individuals who received a copy of Sir Eric's address as well as a copy of his draft resolution, from his Ambassador-at-Large, Dr. Wellington Friday, for review and comment. To assist in progressing this matter through the U.N., I wrote to the Honourable Don Jamieson, Secretary of State for External Affairs, asking that Canada give its full support to Grenada's resolution which was to be presented shortly.

The reply to my letter indicated that Canada was now backing off. The letter said that the writer was " not sure that the United Nations is necessarily the best body in which to conduct research on UFOs (private research organizations might prove better)."

Private research organizations have been operating for up to twenty-five years but due to lack of funds and access to government scientific and technical resources and government information, have been severely limited in what they have been able to accomplish. In my opinion, only an organization sponsored and funded by the U.N. could conduct an adequate world-wide study.

A considerable amount of diplomatic footwork took place in New York over the content of Sir Eric's draft resolution, primarily on the part of the U.S.A. and Great Britain. The U.S. delegation said it could not support the draft resolution because several items were "too demanding". This included a requirement that governments open their files for the study.[11] Evidently, the U.S. Government is not prepared to do this.

The exposure for public scrutiny of classified UFO files of the various governments may likely be what will prevent the U.N. from effectively tackling the UFO problem. The cloak of secrecy

41

hangs heavily over many matters.

In December, 1977, Grenada withdrew its resolution. In its place, Sir Eric circulated a special draft resolution directed at Secretary-General Kurt Waldheim which urged the U.N. to conduct an investigation into the UFO problem and into the prospects for contact with extraterrestrial life. The draft resolution was forwarded to the Member States and the item was placed on the agenda for the 33rd General Assembly in September, 1978.[12]

On July 14th, 1978,Secretary-General Kurt Waldheim met with Sir Eric Gairy and a panel of scientists to discuss a mechanism to facilitate the exchange of UFO information among scientists of various countries.[13] All of the scientists agreed that the UFO phenomenon is real and that an international monitoring system should be established to study it.

At the 33rd Session of the United Nations, on October 12, 1978, Sir Eric again appealed for a U.N. monitoring system for UFOs. The matter was item #126 on the agenda and it was referred to the Special Political Committee, which considered it at meetings on November 27, and December 8, 1978. At the November 27th meeting, Dr. J. Allen Hynek stated:

> There was a growing community of scientists from many countries, especially France and the United States, who had declared an interest in pursuing the challenge presented by the UFO problem and were gathering and analyzing the relevant data. France had assumed a leading role in the scientific approach to the question of UFOs.[14]

At the November meeting, a statement by former U.S. astronaut Gordon Cooper was read. Cooper was supposed to be present as part of Grenada's delegation but was unable to attend. In this statement Cooper said:

> I believe that these extraterrestrial vehicles and their crews are visiting this planet from other planets, which obviously are a little more technically advanced than we are here on earth . . . there are several of us [astronauts] who do believe in UFOs and who have had occasion to see a UFO . . .[15]

The outcome of these meetings was that the Special Political Committee decided by consensus to recommend to the General Assembly the establishment of an agency or a department of the

United Nations for undertaking, co-ordinating and disseminating the results of research into Unidentified Flying Objects and related phenomena. The draft decision went on to recommend that the General Assembly invite interested Member States to take appropriate steps to co-ordinate on a national level scientific research and investigation into extraterrestrial life, including Unidentified Flying Objects and to inform the Secretary-General of the observations, research and evaluation of such activities.

The Committee asked the Secretary-General to transmit the statements of the delegation of Grenada and the relevant documentation to the Committee on the Peaceful Uses of Outer Space so that it may consider them at its 1979 session. The Committee's deliberation would be included in its report which will be considered by the General Assembly at its next session.[16]

In January 1979, the General Assembly adopted this draft decision of the Special Political Committee.[17]

Meanwhile, Coleman VonKeviczky is secretly meeting with several important delegates of powerful nations to attempt to introduce a proposal into the agenda of the U.N. for later this year.[18]

The wheels of the United Nations turn very slowly but we may soon see a global co-ordinating body operating under United Nations auspices, unless certain nations persist in their view that making their UFO files available is still "too demanding".

CHAPTER 6

THE GOVERNMENT FILES

"No studies on UFOs have been carried out by Transport Canada", a senior official with that Department informed me by telephone, "nor does Transport Canada have any regulations regarding UFOs". He followed up this information with the statement that they hold no reports of UFOs from pilots or air traffic controllers.

These statements were little short of amazing considering the well-attested fact that UFOs do approach close to civil aircraft at times and the fact that Transport Canada is responsible for air safety in Canada. Consider the following case where an unknown object flew in formation with an airliner:

An unidentified object was sighted by the Captain and crew of a Capital Airlines DC8 jet at approximately 4:15 a.m. on October 11, 1974 when enroute westerly to Gander International Airport. The aircraft was at 7500 feet at the time.

The object pulled alongside the big DC8 flashing red and white lights. It maintained a course parallel with the DC8 until the object disappeared in cloud cover approximately five miles from Gander Airport. The big jet was travelling at approximately 290 miles per hour and the object continued to maintain the speed of the DC8 but at times would speed up just a little ahead of the jet and return alongside.

The Captain and First Officer both confirmed that the object **was not an aircraft**. Air Traffic Control Gander confirmed there were no other aircraft in the area.[1]

Transport Canada stated in 1976 that there have been no instances of intrusions into controlled airspace by UFOs that they are aware of.[2] If they are unaware of the foregoing case, **why** don't they know?

Here are other interesting cases of which Transport Canada should be aware:

Quebec Air flight 650 aircrew sighted an object at the end of runway 14 at Sept Iles, Quebec on November 15, 1967. The object was very bright, larger than a star, stationary, at an unknown altitude. The weather was clear. This case was logged in the Chief Air Traffic Controller's log.[3]

A Scandinavian Airlines Captain flying 35 to 40 miles southeast of Quebec City in July 1974 reported a triangular-shaped object moving southwesterly. Bagotville reported radio frequency interference during the sighting.[4]

Are our "experts" in Transport Canada really unaware of the facts of UFO activity or are they covering up? How can Transport Canada possibly be concerned with air safety while ignoring UFOs?

I asked to see the files which were maintained by the Department of Transport (DOT) in the 1950s when Wilbert B. Smith was actively engaged in UFO work (see Chap. 7). "Can't help you", this same official said, "but I suggest you call Mr. Jones, (name changed by author) acting Chief of Operations. He may be able to help you."

I dialed Mr. Jones' number and told him what I wanted. "Will check and call you back" he answered. The next day my phone rang and Jones was on the line. "All our UFO files were transferred to the Department of Communications (DOC) when that department was formed in 1969" he informed me. "They took over certain responsibilities from our department so we transferred all relevant files". He kindly gave me the number to call in DOC.

I quickly made an appointment to visit the Department of Communications.[5] Here I was given full co-operation.

The dormant DOC files were brought up from the storage section of the basement, and together with the one current volume, I was allowed to peruse them at my leisure. There are four volumes bearing one file number, all unclassified.[6] However volume 3 could not be located after an extensive search. A check by phone several weeks later revealed it still could not be located. It was presumed to have been misfiled somewhere in the basement storage room, as it had not been logged out. I was therefore able to view only volumes 1, 2 and 4.

Volume 1,[7] contained essentially a large number of letters of inquiry from private citizens, plus some sighting reports and miscellaneous correspondence but nothing of particular interest other than the memo of June 25, 1954 cited as reference 14 of Chapter 7. This volume covers the period October 1953 to April 1956.

Volume 2 covers the period from April 1956 to March 1966 and contains, again, a number of sighting reports by private citizens and one from a CP Air pilot. The usual letter of acknowledgment of sighting reports, signed by Wilbert B. Smith, says "This department does not make any analysis of these sightings."

An interesting letter[8] to a private citizen, from the RCMP says:

> Over a period of years, certain information was received by this Force relating to UFOs. Investigations were made and the findings forwarded to the Chairman, Defence Research Board, DND.

Another interesting letter,[9] from Defence Research Board to the same citizen states:

> DRB has not undertaken to investigate sightings of UFOs and is not associated with any projects which may have been reported in the press.

Again, a letter from Wilbert B. Smith to the same citizen,[10] has the following to say:

> We came to the conclusion that there was about 90% probability that the objects were real and a 60% probability that they were extraterrestrial. However, these conclusions are not official and are entirely those of the small group who worked with me in the analysis of the data.

The current file,[11] contains nothing of special interest—simply letters of inquiry and the standard replies.

Returning to Volume 1, I found right at the beginning of the file, a note concerning the existence of two more UFO files, classified SECRET.[12] The DOC file staff denied any knowledge of these files and after checking the file index, confirmed no record of them in the Department of Communications.

However, two months later, in a phone call to check further on these missing files, I was informed that one secret file was in fact held by DOC and was now classified as confidential.[13] In further checking with Transport Canada I was assured that both secret files were transferred to DOC but DOC nevertheless argued that one of the two[14] had never been transferred. There was still no record of the location of this file. Concerning the now confidential file on Project Magnet, in a subsequent letter to the Minister of Communications I asked that this file be declassified and made available to me. The Department, in its reply, now denied holding such a file.[15] Regardless of whether they were held by DOC or Transport Canada, the fact remains that there were classified UFO files and no way the public could gain access to their contents. Here at last was definite evidence that the Government of Canada was withholding UFO information.

On a subsequent visit in 1979, I was presented with the files I originally reviewed, as well as, surprisingly, two others! One was the previously-missing volume 3. An interesting letter from the Chief of Information Services, Department of Transport, informed an inquirer:

> The existence of such objects [UFOs] has not been officially recognized and is not, therefore, an administrative problem insofar as the Canadian Government is concerned. For these reasons, the Minister has formed no opinion on the matter.[16]

The remainder of this volume is essentially inquiries and standard replies.

Early in 1978 I wrote to the Minister of Communications seeking declassification of the confidential file referred to previously but the reply stated that such a file did not exist! This was despite the fact that internal memos in the unclassified files proved it did exist.

On my second visit to DOC, in 1979, this very file was presented to me as one of the two surprises noted above. Now, however, this file was re-identified as volume 5 of the main series. It has now been declassified.[17] The file now contains material bearing the file numbers of the two secret files which DOT insisted were transferred to DOC as well as the number of the confidential file which DOC denied possessing. Whether all the original material from those classified files is now in this new file can only be guessed at. In any event, here at last was formerly-classified material on UFOs. If UFOs do not exist, why the secrecy?

The files which create the greatest current interest are those of the National Research Council (NRC), a quasi-government body, probably because NRC is still in the UFO business as the custodian of current sighting reports, and supposedly having investigation responsibility. But NRC scientists say that scientific investigations cannot be fruitful on the basis of narrative reports. Physical evidence is required, they insist. Dr. Peter Millman, a noted Canadian astronomer and former "UFO Chief" at NRC has admitted that, with respect to meteors, it is only by receiving reports of observations "from a large number of people that we can make a satisfactory scientific study of these objects." [18] This is confirmed in a statement by Dr. Ian Halliday of NRC where he says "The MORP (Meteorite Observation and Recovery Project) Project relies on public feedback. . ."[19] This being the case, why do these same scientists insist that they cannot conduct a scientific investigation of UFOs based only on the testimony of witnesses?

An interesting observation is that despite the claims of NRC scientists that flying saucers do not exist and all unusual aerial sightings can be rationally explained, some of them, including Dr. Millman, attend public meetings where a certain woman outlines her many claimed abductions by space beings in flying saucers. Why the interest in such claims when they "know" flying saucers are non-existant?

How does one explain the following? On March 24, 1975, I had a puzzling telephone conversation with Dr. Brown (name changed by author) of the Herzberg Institute of Astrophysics, NRC. Our discussion centred on a reported UFO landing near Maniwaki, Quebec. The landing was supposed to have occurred in a remote valley, in front of large steel doors in the stone cliff on one side. Photographs showed two beings standing near the saucer, with the huge doors in the background.

I informed Dr. Brown that I had recently been made aware of the story and had seen the photos and hoped to proceed with an investigation as soon as possible. Dr. Brown told me that he was most interested and also had plans to visit the site. I proposed we make the trip together and he agreed this was a reasonable proposal and he would call me when ready to make the trip. I asked Dr. Brown what he thought of this case and he replied that it was "either a hoax or the greatest scientific discovery of all time". Subsequently, it turned out the story and the photos were a hoax.

The curious aspect of this episode is that the NRC was even interested in a supposed landing where occupants were involved. The "vault" in the cliff face made this case seem very like science fiction. If UFOs do not exist, why did NRC exhibit distinct interest in such a claim?

By displaying interest and intention to investigate, they acknowledged the possibility the story was true. Such an acknowledgement is contrary to the accepted scientific viewpoint.

This episode, and the foregoing about NRC scientists attending lectures where claims of contacts and abductions are made, plus other things which don't quite fit in, raise real questions about the true views of NRC concerning UFOs.

A New Zealand airline pilot named Bruce Cathie wrote a book titled **Harmonic 695** in which he made a quantum leap in UFO research. His theory involves the relationship of nuclear explosions to a grid surrounding Earth which is, according to Cathie, used by UFOs for various purposes including propulsion. His theory was brilliant and his evidence impressive.

I sent a copy of this intriguing book to Dr. Schneider, President of NRC, with the request that Canadian scientists give their opinion on its contents. I felt that as Cathie had presented such a well-researched and documented case it was incumbent upon science to show that he is wrong, if indeed he is.

I finally received a reply which informed me that "the limited resources of NRC prevent it from undertaking in any meaningful way" the investigation I requested.

Two alternatives are open. Either NRC was not interested; or they were interested and may already have been aware of all this, but would not admit it. Take your choice.

In 1968, when the Department of National Defence (DND) concluded that UFOs did not pose a threat to national security, it turned over its responsibility, along with files, to NRC.

The files are identified as the "Non-Meteoritic Sighting Files", not "UFO Files". Sighting reports of aerial objects referred to NRC are scrutinized to determine if they were of meteors. If so, they are handled as such. Any reports which were **not** of meteors are then placed in this 'residue file'—non-meteoritic sightings.

This leaves us with a great many reports of things which could be anything—except meteors. It is important to realize that all reports are not of genuine UFOs. In the first place, most of these reports have not been investigated to determine if they can be identified as anything other than meteors. The reports, in nearly all cases, are simply filed and forgotten about. **Some** of these reports have been carefully investigated however without being able to identify the phenomena concerned. A few of these cases have been referred to previously. The NRC-originated sighting report files are numbered according to an NRC system. There is a separate series for the DND reports.

To view these files,[20] an appointment must be made.[21] One will find a file cabinet stuffed with bulging folders containing the report documentation, and two file drawers of index cards identifying the reports by serial number and date and place of the reported sighting.[22]

Looking first at the oldest reports we find those from DND which consist of a collection numbered from 001 to 269. However, numbers 177 to 199 are "not allocated". The reason for this is not clear, as the gap does not occur at the end of a year but in the middle of November 1967. A check with Dr. A. G. McNamara, who is in charge of the Planetary Sciences Section of the Herzberg Institute of Astrophysics, and now responsible for the 'UFO files', disclosed that they do not know, as, of course, the files were the property of DND at the time the gap occurred. He, and Dr. Peter Millman who had McNamara's job at the time the files were transferred "guess" that it was "an administrative adjustment to tidy up the file" as there had been great commotion and a great deal of paper work involved with the Michalak case (see Chapter 3) which became DND case No. 200.[23]

Also, 9 DND reports are missing with no explanation. Were reports bearing these serial numbers removed by DND prior to transfer? There are also 6 reports with a suffix "A". The total number of DND reports held is 216, covering the period 1965 to 1968 with the exception of # 044 dated 1962 which was a telephoned report from New York. Some of the reports are not sighting cases, but are simply DND internal correspondence on UFOs in general.

The total number of reports in the Non-Meteoritic Sighting Files for the years 1965 to 1978 inclusive, in addition to the 216 DND reports, is approximately 1900.

These files at NRC are available to those interested but any researcher viewing them is required to sign a statement undertaking to keep confidential any personal name or names learned from the files, without prior permission from the person or persons concerned. This routine is reasonable as many reports were submitted in confidence.

We have seen that the files at NRC including those transferred from DND commence in 1965. Where are the DND reports for the pre-1965 sightings? I will return to this question later.

In addition to the sighting report files, there were two volumes of general correspondence.[24] These contain general inquiries from the public as well as interdepartmental correspondence. I found nothing of particular interest in these files. They are current and start about 1965, but as they are arranged alphabetically rather than chronologically it would require more time to determine the precise date of commencement.

Now let us turn to the Department of National Defence. Prior to 1965, Air Defence Command (ADC) in co-operation with North American Air Defence Command (NORAD) was the recognized defence agency primarily concerned with UFOs. However, as a result of numerous investigations, ADC concluded that there was no evidence to suggest that UFOs posed a threat to national security and the responsibility for UFO investigation was transferred to Canadian Forces Headquarters (CFHQ).[25] However, it is also of interest that the Honourable James Richardson, as Minister of National Defence, stated that he did "not wish to comment on UFOs and National Security as the subject is inconclusive and surrounded by far too much speculation".[26]

In view of the duplication in recording systems at NRC for the period of 1965 to 1968, it appears that both DND and NRC were collecting reports during this period. But what happened to the DND sighting reports prior to 1965? It appears, from DND correspondence, that these files were destroyed by ADC "in accordance with normal disposal instructions. . .as their files would have served no useful purpose to CFHQ".[27] However, I have also been informed that the files **were** transferred to NRC. This information originated with the DND Records Management Office. However, NRC denies that any pre-1965 files were transferred.[28]

I was also informed that a number of UFO files are held by DND at the Public Archives Records Centre.[29]

My attempt to view these files met with considerable difficulty. The National Archives had informed me in a check with them that no DND files are held there, and confirmed there are DND files in the Public Archives Records Centre even though DND retains control over them. I was informed by the National Archives that files do not go to the Archives until they become of historical interest which is not normally until after thirty years, when they may be made public. The unit to contact in DND, I was told, would be the Directorate of History. I called there and my request to view the files was met with some trepidation.

"You can't see these files because the names of witnesses are confidential" I was told. "But NRC lets the public see their files" I countered, "and so does DOC so why can't I see yours?" "Well, it just isn't our policy" said Mr. Chaplin on the other end of the line. "We have never let anyone see them before". "Then it's about time you did", I replied. Mr. Chaplin promised to look into the matter to see what could be arranged. Clearance from higher authority would be required.

A few weeks later, a letter arrived from Mr. Chaplin stating that my request had been considered with the following findings:

1. The file titles include the phrase "unidentified objects", omitting the word "flying", and the files therefore contain a considerable amount of irrelevant material, some of which properly bears security classifications.

2. Besides the reports of sightings, the files contain internal departmental correspondence which are exempt from release under Cabinet Directive No. 45.

3. Each report includes the name and address of the observer, and, since the information was given to the department on the understanding that the observer would not be publicly identified, the reports cannot be released in their present form.

4. Some of the reports were made through RCMP channels and cannot be released without the concurrence of that force.

The following procedure is therefore proposed:

1. Photocopy the reports made to this department and place these copies in a new file.

2. Obliterate the name and address of the observer in each report.

3. Place the file in this directorate's document collection for future reference.

You will then be able to see the information provided to this department by the people who actually saw the phenomena.[30]

Faced with this situation I had no choice but to agree to the terms. It was that or nothing. The names of the witnesses are unimportant for my purposes. It is the events which concern me.

Dormant files may be retained by government departments as long as they have use for them. Alternatively, if departments have storage problems these files may be placed in what is known as the Public Archives Records Centre, located at Tunney's Pasture in Ottawa's West End. The only access to files at Tunney's Pasture is by the departments owning the files, and only they can draw the files from the Records Centre. Hence, DND withdrew the UFO files to make them available to me.

Nineteen months were to pass before DND finally had their files ready for me to see and I am certain I would never have been allowed to see them at all if I had not persisted.

The file numbers did not entirely match those identified to me in Note 29, but consisted of one file formerly unclassified, two formerly confidential and one formerly secret.[31] One file, classified Secret, which I was told in writing existed, has now, I am told, been destroyed.[32]

All these files were "sanitized" (the elimination of information not collected by DND and the excision of the names of civilian observers from the reports). In this form, the files are unclassified and open to the public. All material consists of photocopies of material in the original files. The original files still exist in the custody of NDRMS (National Defence Records Management Section).

These files commence in July 1947 and contain a large number of sighting reports, but little investigative material. They do not go beyond August 1961. The only item of special interest was a 1950 report of a visit to USAF Headquarters by an RCAF Intelligence Officer in which it was concluded that flying saucers are no threat to security of the U.S.A. and represent misinterpretations, mass hysteria and hoaxes.

I was informed that the ADC files pre-1965 were transferred to NRC and that the CFHQ files for the period 1961 to 1965 "may have been destroyed". Their whereabouts is unknown.

John Magor, a thoroughly reliable investigator, and the publisher and editor of a very reputable magazine, **Canadian UFO Report,** reports in this book that an RCAF officer investigating a sighting in 1964, visited the witness with a briefcase full of UFO photos for the purpose of comparison. The officer, who was known to the witness, stressed that despite their acquaintance he would deny the visit if it was made public.[33] Where does DND keep these photos hidden?

No doubt they are in the Defence Photo Interpretation Centre in Ottawa. I do know that this unit has analyzed photos of reported UFOs in the past as I was personally involved with one of these cases some years ago while serving in the Armed Forces.

What about cases investigated by the RCMP? In many instances RCMP officers are first on the scene after a report of a UFO sighting. In a number of cases they have been witnesses to sightings. In my check with RCMP Headquarters a spokesman assured me that it is routine procedure for all such reports to be sent to NRC. Certainly there are RCMP reports in the NRC files. Whether they all reach that central point may be another matter. I have no way of determining this.

However, it is interesting to note that when DND turned over its responsibility to NRC, the RCMP asked for all RCMP reports on UFOs to be returned to them, and not be passed to other government agencies. This request was complied with.[34] I have seen a four-page list of RCMP reports which were removed from these files and returned to the RCMP.

The now defunct Information Canada (Infocan) proved its inability to locate, or admit the existence of UFO files within the government. Infocan was the government agency responsible for answering public inquiries where several departments or agencies are involved.

I had written to Infocan seeking to identify the departments or agencies maintaining UFO files.[35] Upon this first attempt, my letter was simply referred to NRC and Dr. McNamara told me nothing because I was "already aware of our procedures and the contents of our files" and he could "not add anything further to what you already know at first hand".[36]

The Honourable John Munro, the minister responsible for Infocan, was my next target as I complained of this shabby treatment. Again, I was equally specific about the information I sought. He informed me in his reply that "five departments and agencies were contacted but no trace of any dormant files on Unidentified Flying Objects could be found".[37] Note the lack of reference to current files which I can only assume was deliberate.

As seen previously, I was successful in tracking down dormant files in both DOC and DND, as well as current files.

In a letter from the Department of External Affairs, I was informed that "the Canadian Government does not underestimate the seriousness of the question of UFOs and this matter is being kept under consideration and study in a number of departments and agencies".[38]

Why the apparent lack of interest in UFOs by the Ministry of Transport? Why the "disappearance" of secret files? Why was I given such a run-around in trying to uncover the contents of government files on UFOs?

I am thoroughly convinced that the Government of Canada was engaged in a cover-up operation. Of course, the lack of information could simply have been incompetence and plain bumbling on the part of all Ministers of the Crown and public servants concerned, but I cannot honestly believe that all the high officials I contacted were really that incompetent. The only explanation, in my view, is a deliberate cover-up. My many years of badgering the government on this leaves me no alternative conclusion. For a number of years I deliberately avoided such a conclusion in the hope that I was wrong. I can no longer avoid it.

Cover-up of UFO facts is not unique to Canada. It exists around the world and a very large number of documents have recently been released by the FBI and CIA in the U.S.A. under the Freedom of Information Act, which is positive proof of secrecy having been maintained over a period of thirty years.

Ufologists are familiar with the case of a 3000 pound mass of metal reported to have fallen from the sky under very strange circumstances near Les Ecureuils on the St. Lawrence River in 1960. Government scientists are the first to admit this was not a meteorite and claim it is foundry slag.[39] However, at least eight separate analyses have been undertaken on samples of this metal and all results differ significantly. One university professor said he was "disturbed" by the results. A full report of this interesting case, written by myself, will appear soon in the **Encyclopedia of UFOs** to be published by Doubleday (New York).

Much interesting information has now been brought into the open, however, with the release of the Canadian Government files referred to. More facts from these files will be brought to light in the next chapter.

CHAPTER 7

PROJECTS MAGNET AND SECOND STOREY

"We are faced with a substantial probability of the real existence of extraterrestrial space vehicles" was the conclusion of a leading Canadian radio engineer in his report on a three year study of UFOs.

Established in 1950 by the Department of Transport, PROJECT MAGNET was the first Canadian government investigation into UFOs, according to available records. It was under the direction of Mr. Wilbert B. Smith, Senior Radio Engineer, Broadcast and Measurements Section of that Department. Mr. Smith was already internationally recognized in his field of radio communications, held a number of patents and had received a number of awards for his work in radio. He was a graduate of the University of British Columbia, having received both the B.Sc. and M.Sc. degrees in Electrical Engineering. He had represented Canada at the Canada-U.S. FM Broadcasting Agreement in 1947 as well as at other international conferences. He was in charge of establishing a network of ionospheric measurement stations throughout Canada.

Project Magnet was a small program using Department of Transport (DOT) facilities with the assistance of other government organizations including the Defence Research Board (DRB) and National Research Council (NRC).

Much has been written and spoken about Project Magnet over the years but a large proportion of this has been misleading, incomplete or inaccurate. In this chapter I will attempt to set the record straight, using official government documents as sources of my information. The information in some of these documents has never before been made public.

In addition to the government files I have reviewed, I have been privileged to obtain certain other material and information for which specific references cannot be cited due to the need to protect my sources.

The project was an outgrowth of work already being done by Smith and a small group of engineers on the collapse of the Earth's magnetic field as a source of energy. It was believed that

57

Wilbert B. Smith

"Flying Saucers" were operating on magnetic principles and it seemed that this work might explain the saucers' operation. Smith had been informed by highly-placed sources that flying saucers are indeed real, that they are almost certainly of extraterrestrial origin and that they operate on a magnetic principle. Just how this principle actually operated was unknown.

Early in 1950, a book by Frank Scully (**Behind the Flying Saucers**) claimed that flying saucers had crashed in the USA and that the US Air Force had retrieved them along with the dead bodies of their occupants. Although some people have claimed that Scully's book was a hoax, Smith was informed by a certain top American Scientist who was deeply involved in UFO research for the US Government, that "the facts reported in the book are substantially correct".

On November 21, 1950, Smith submitted a proposal to the Controller of Telecommunications to set up a special project within the Department. He stated in his proposal that his group believed they were on the track of something which may well prove to be the introduction to a new technology. It appeared that their work in geomagnetics might well be the linkage between our technology and the technology by which the saucers are designed and operated.

The study of UFOs, or flying saucers as they were called in those days, was of tremendous interest at top levels of the US Government, and Smith was informed that the matter was the most highly classified subject in that government, rating higher even than the H-bomb. Top officials were aware of their reality, he was also told.

Smith had discussed the work of his group with Dr. O. M. Solandt, Chairman, Defence Research Board, who agreed that work on geomagnetic energy should go forward as rapidly as possible and offered full co-operation of his Board, according to Smith's proposal.

The project was classified, and for several reasons. The exchange of information with other parallel classified projects could thereby be facilitated; scientific personnel working along unorthodox lines prefer to work in camera until their results can be proven; and furthermore, in the event that a new technology should be uncovered, its implications would have to be carefully assessed before pertinent information could be made public.

There has been misunderstanding and confusion over whether Smith's project was an official one. Numerous statements from the government have denied that it was. Let's examine this situation. The files of the former DOT covering the period of the 1950s contain an undated statement for the Minister of Transport to deliver in the House of Commons. The pertinent part of this statement says that

> This entire program . . . is being carried on . . . with official approval and authority to make use of existing facilities.[1]

The full statement appears as Annex 2.

In 1963 HANSARD tells us that a statement was made in the House of Commons by Mr. Dupuis:

> Between December 1950 and August 1954 a small program of investigation in the field of geomagnetics was carried out by the then telecommunications division of the Department of Transport with a view to obtaining, if possible, some physical information or facts which might help to explain the phenomenon which was generally referred to as unidentified flying objects. Mr. W. B. Smith was the engineer in charge of this program.[2]

In 1964 I was told by the Department of Transport:

> . . . at no time has this Department carried out research in the field of unidentified flying objects . . . The Department did not take part in any of his [Smith's] research work nor did Mr. Smith provide the Department with any useful information arising out of his work.[3]

In 1966, Dr. William D. Howe, MP, wrote to J. R. Baldwin, Deputy Minister of Transport, seeking information on Project Magnet. In reply, a Mr. D. A. McDougal answered that:

> . . .these activities [Smith's] were purely a personal hobby of his and we have no Departmental information on the subject.[4]

A 1968 memorandum in the National Research Council files signed by Dr. Peter M. Millman, at that time Head of Upper Atmosphere Research, states:

> I have been informed by the Department of Transport that although Project Magnet was officially authorized by the Depart-

ment, work on this project was carried out almost entirely by Mr. W. B. Smith and was in the nature of a spare time activity.[5]

Four months later, Dr. Millman stated:

The project was a personal one carried out by Mr. Smith with the knowledge of his department, but without any official government sponsorship.[6]

These statements are typical examples of what the public and Parliament was being told regarding the status of Project Magnet.

However, Department of Transport internal correspondence (see Annex 3, paragraph 1) makes the whole matter clear as the statement is made that:

Project Magnet was established November 21, 1950 by authority of Commander C. P. Edwards, then Deputy Minister of Transport for Air Services.

The files of the Department of Communications show that Smith's proposal was dated November 21, 1950, and that formal approval was given by Edwards on December 2, 1950.

It is quite clear that despite the fact the public was being told that Project Magnet was not a government project, it in fact was, at least for a period of time. The situation changed later.

Smith's program consisted of two parts. The first part was the collecting of as much high quality data as possible, analyzing it, and where possible drawing conclusions from it. The second part consisted of a systematic questioning of all our basic concepts in the hopes of turning up a discrepancy which might prove to be the key to a new technology.[7] He also developed ideas for measuring the reliability of observational data and using these measurements to rate the probability that a given report could be accepted as a real observation.

In 1950, an article intended for publication in an American magazine was written by Major Donald E. Keyhoe, U.S. Marine Corps (Retired), later Director of the National Investigations Committee on Aerial Phenomena (NICAP) on the reality of the saucers. This article was in fact partly ghost-written by Wilbert B. Smith and cleared by the Chairman, Defence Research Board of Canada. What Smith wrote correctly reflected the work of Magnet to date so it gave credence to the Canadian part of the article. There are also definite indications that clearance was given at a very high level in the US. If Canadian approval was sought for an American-originated article it would seem certain that similar US clearance must have been obtained. This matter of security clearances puts an official stamp of approval on the contents of the article which stated that saucers operated on a magnetic principle.

In January 1951, Smith stated in a letter to a senior member of the Canadian Embassy staff in Washington, in which he was reporting on progress, that three engineers and two technicians were working full time on Project Magnet. This demolishes repeated government statements that the project was simply a part-time activity on the part of Smith.

High security was attached to the flying saucer matter and only two staff members of the Embassy in Washington were even allowed to discuss the matter.

Smith submitted an interim report to his department in June, 1952 in which he stated that it appeared evident that flying saucers are emissaries from some other civilization and actually do operate on magnetic principles.[8] This complete report appears as Annex 3.

On August 10, 1953, Smith filed a further report on the project and he concluded that we are faced with a substantial probability of the real existence of extra-terrestrial vehicles and that such vehicles must of necessity use a technology considerably in advance of what we have.[9]

It will also serve a useful purpose to include the complete report in this book so readers may decide for themselves whether Smith reached a valid conclusion from the evidence presented. This report appears as Annex 4.

The Government has also consistently denied that Smith's report was an official one, claiming that it simply represented his own views and not those of the Government. However, it should be noted that the Government never made an official statement either accepting or rejecting the conclusions of the report. It simply disclaimed any official status for the report. Smith himself has stated that this report represented simply the views of himself and his small group, and that his report had not been endorsed by the Government. Neither was it rejected.

The report stands on the reputation of Smith as a very capable and careful investigator whose ability was beyond dispute and who for years afterwards continued to represent his department before the House of Commons Broadcasting Committee.

On November 13, 1953, the world's first "flying saucer sighting station" was placed in operation by Smith. Located at Shirleys Bay, ten miles northwest of Ottawa, it consisted of some highly sophisticated instrumentation for the purpose of detecting flying saucers. The instruments were located in a small shack near the DOT Ionosphere Station on Defence Research Board property. There was a gamma ray counter to detect the presence of radioactive or cosmic radiation; a magnetometer which would register variations or disturbances in the earth's magnetic field; a radio receiver to detect the presence of radio noise; and a recording gravimeter to detect any variation in the earth's gravitational pull. The four instruments produced traces on a multiple-pen graphical recorder, the charts from which were scrutinized from time to time for any disturbance which might appear. These instruments were left over from a previous program of radio and skywave recording and were specially adapted for UFO detection.

Government scientists were reluctant to admit publicly that they regarded stories of flying saucers as anything but utter nonsense and were inclined to dismiss the very existence of the saucer station with a snort and a sweep of the hand. On the very day the station went into operation, Dr. O. M. Solandt, Chairman of the Defence Research Board, was quoted as saying reports of the station's establishment were completely untrue. Later he claimed he actually had said such a station was not being operated by his department and he personally had no knowledge of its existence.[10] In fact, the building was loaned to Smith by the Defence Research Board.[11]

On August 8th, 1954 at 3.01 p.m., the instrumentation in the Shirleys Bay station registered a very definite disturbance, quite different from disturbances registered by passing aircraft. In Smith's words "the gravimeter went wild". All evidence indicated that a UFO had flown within feet of the station. Smith and his colleagues were alerted to this event by alarm systems connected to the instrument panel. Unfortunately, the area was clouded in at the time and they could see nothing which was causing the commotion with the instruments. Whatever was up there was hidden in the cloud. However, the event was recorded

**The world's first flying saucer observatory
at Shirleys Bay, near Ottawa, Canada.**

on the chart paper as evidence of some sort of major disturbance, quite distinct from that of even the largest aircraft.

Two days later, DOT announced it was dropping Project Magnet. How could this be possible when the evidence waited for had now been obtained, despite lack of visual confirmation?

The records show that on August 10th, 1954, the Controller of Telecommunications issued a form letter (a note added that this could also be used as a press release) which admitted that DOT had been engaged in a study of UFOs for three and one-half years, that considerable data was collected and analyzed but it had not been possible to reach any definite conclusion, and since new data simply confirmed existing data there seemed little point in carrying the investigation any further **on an official level** (emphasis added). This release went on to state that DOT would discontinue any further study of UFOs and that Project Magnet would be dropped. It ended by adding that Wilbert Smith would continue to receive and catalogue future data "on a purely unofficial basis".[12] A memo was sent to Smith the same day directing him to discontinue the DOT activities.

Here we have, in addition to further confirmation that Project Magnet was an official DOT project, a startling turn of events by the announcement itself, and its timing. Two days! Just enough time to call hasty meetings to consider the importance of the event at Shirleys Bay, decide what to do, and prepare a statement for the public.

But it made no sense to shut it all down now that they had some scientific confirmation of what DOT was looking for. In personal correspondence, Smith stated that there were a number of reasons behind this decision but they **did not include lack of results**. (Emphasis added). Did it all move to a higher level and go behind more security? Smith tells us that as the project proceeded it ran into difficulties from the press:

> The program was plagued by well-meaning but misguided journalists who were looking for spectacular copy which could be turned to political account to such an extent that both those who were working on the project, and the Department of Transport found themselves in an embarrassed position. Consequently, when the Project Magnet report was made and permission sought to extend the scope of the investigation through federal financial support, the decision was finally made in 1954 that this would not

be advisable in the face of the publicity from which the whole project has suffered.[13]

However, we also find that the **decision** to discontinue the project as an official government-sponsored project was actually made in June 1954, as the DOT files show that Smith was to be told

> . . . that he can continue in his own free time, not on Departmental time. He may continue to use Departmental equipment not otherwise in use. . .[14]

This leaves us with a puzzling picture of what was going on behind the scenes. To recap, the press was creating problems for the government and in June 1954 it was decided to terminate the project, officially, but to permit Smith to continue unofficially and on his own time. On August 8th, a UFO was evidently tracked on the sensitive instruments at Shirleys Bay, then on August 10th the government hastened to announce publicly that the project had been discontinued. Surely this evidence should have justified keeping the project going officially. However, it is significant that it **was** kept going, even though unofficially. The situation seems to indicate an official cover-up by leading the public to believe the government was no longer involved or interested.

Smith stated in a private letter:

> . . . when certain government people came face to face with the reality of the space people, and realized that there wasn't anything they could do about it, they promptly closed their eyes and hoped that the whole business would fade out and go away.

During much of the period of Project Magnet's official activity, which dealt with the physics of flying saucers, a parallel project was underway in which Wilbert Smith was also involved.

In April, 1952, the federal government set up a committee representing a number of departments, and code-named it - PROJECT SECOND STOREY. This consisted of a group of scientists and military officers who met periodically to consider the UFO problem and to recommend government action.

This group was set up at a meeting on April 22, 1952 chaired by Dr. O. M. Solandt, Chairman of the Defence Research Board.

The following persons were nominated and agreed to serve on the Committee:

> Dr. Peter M. Millman (chairman), Dominion Observatory.
> Group Captain D. M. Edwards, Directorate of Air Intelligence.
> LCOL. E. H. Webb, DMOP.
> Commander J. C. Pratt, Directorate of Naval Intelligence.
> Flight Lt. V L. Bradley, Defence Research Board.
> Mr. Wilbert B. Smith, Department of Transport.
> Mr. H. C. Oatway, (secretary), Defence Research Board.

This committee was "to prepare a brief of instructions for observers, examine interrogation procedures and to get a consolidated and pertinent series of questions."[15] The minutes of the organizing meeting as well as those of Project Second Storey which it set up, were classified "Confidential".[16]

According to the minutes made available to me by NRC, it would seem that only five meetings of the Second Storey Committee were held, the first being on April 24, 1952 and the last on March 9, 1953.

At first it was agreed to call the work of this Committee "Project Theta". However, at the second meeting it was agreed to adopt the name "Project Second Storey".

The minutes of the first meeting of Second Storey record that a report by the RCAF relative to the USAF project on flying saucers was tabled. This report was to be duplicated by the RCAF and copies passed to the secretary for distribution to the Committee members.[17]

This report was not attached to the minutes made available to me. Government sources always insist that no information is being withheld from the public, so why was this report not made available?

At the third meeting, the Committee approved a form titled "Project Second Storey Sighting Report". This standard form was apparently to be used by all persons when investigating a UFO report. An information or instruction pamphlet was also prepared for distribution with Sighting Report Forms, in two parts:

> Part I — Information for Guidance in reporting on unknown flying objects
> Part II — Description of normal phenomena which might cause reports of unidentified aerial objects.

It is clear from the minutes that Second Storey was not inten-ded for the purpose of actually investigating sighting reports. Its purpose was really to facilitate this work by others, hence the development of the Sighting Report Form and the accompanying pamphlet.

Smith reported on an experiment carried out under DOT auspices in an endeavour to obtain data relative to the accuracy of reports. A large meteorological balloon, approximately twelve feet in diameter, to which was attached a thirty second magnesium flare, was released from the Central Experimental Farm.[18] No advance notice was given to the press. As of the fourth meeting DOT had not received any queries relating to the experiment.[19] Perhaps no one noticed this device in the air. On the other hand, perhaps people **can** tell the difference between a lighted balloon and a flying saucer!

A further document was developed by Smith and approved by the Committee, in the form of "Weighting Factors for Analysis of Sighting Reports". In the analysis of sighting reports it was fairly obvious that different reports would have widely different values from the viewpoint of reliability, confirmation and lucidity. A formula was devised giving approximately the same significance to each of these factors and derived from numerical values assigned to the answers given to the various questions on the Sighting Report Form.[20]

Also, a Record Card and a Record Instruction Card were designed for the purpose of maintaining adequate records of sightings reported on the Sighting Report Forms.

At the fifth meeting, the chairman outlined his discussions with the Chairman of the Defence Research Board on the future activities of this Committee. It was pointed out that evidence to date did not seem to warrant an all-out investigation by the Canadian Services but it might be well to continue to collect at some central location all forms which may be submitted to the Services. For the present at least, it was considered unnecessary for that Committee or any other section of DND to undertake a detailed analysis of the reports received to date. However, the Committee, the minutes made clear, should retain its existence and hold meetings at the discretion of the chairman. Arrange-ments were being made to bring Captain Ruppelt, head of the US Air Force's Project Blue Book, to Ottawa to brief the Committee.

It was also agreed that a separate file on sightings would be maintained by DSI (Director of Scientific Intelligence, DRB) who would henceforth act as the central agency, and reports received through the various services would be forwarded to DSI for filing. It was not intended that DSI would complete a Record Card system.

It was considered that the next committee meeting need not be held until DOT had completed an analysis of the sightings to date or whenever other members had data which might warrant the calling of a meeting.[21]

There were no further minutes available to indicate whether any subsequent meetings were held. In view of the statement that the Committee should retain its existence, and the fact that there was unfinished business, caused me to suspect that further meetings were held, the minutes of which have not been made public.

Consider the following facts. Meeting No. 5 was held on March 9, 1953 at which it was agreed to meet again on an undetermined date, after a DOT analysis was completed. Wilbert Smith was conducting this analysis for the Department. In August 1953, Smith submitted his Project Magnet Report to the Controller of Telecommunications, DOT. This was obviously the report the Committee was waiting for. I have been informed by a reliable source that this report went as high as Prime Minister Louis St. Laurent who held it for three months.

Smith concluded that we were probably being visited by interplanetary spacecraft. This conclusion had tremendous implications, yet we have nothing on it from Project Second Storey. Why? I cannot believe that the Second Storey group did not consider this report important enough to justify a meeting to discuss it. It can only be concluded that further meetings were held, the minutes of which remain classified by the government.

Strangely enough, recent correspondence with Dr. Allen McNamara of NRC prompted the statement by him (without having been asked the question) that the Project Magnet Report was submitted to the Project Second Storey Committee in 1953. So there we have it. Where are the minutes that show this? He went on to state:

> Mr. Smith's conclusions were not supported by his own Department or by the Second Storey Committee.[22]

The last document in the Second Storey file summarizes this work of the Committee and ends with the following statement:

> The Committee as a whole has felt that owing to the impossibility of checking independently the details of the majority of the sightings, most of the observational material does not lend itself to a scientific method of investigation.[23]

This is a rather odd statement as science consists to a large extent of a search for patterns. Many patterns have been discovered in UFO behaviour as discussed elsewhere in this book. Why was Second Storey not interested in searching for these? The file ends abruptly with no satisfactory explanation. Could it be that Second Storey went "underground" after receiving Smith's report with his startling conclusion? This could account for the unsatisfactory situation faced in attempting to get UFO information from the government.

Not surprisingly, the minutes of one further meeting of Project Second Storey have recently been made available to me by a private source. These are in the form of a draft and are undated, but a government transmittal slip is attached, dated March 15, 1954. I infer from this and from internal evidence of the minutes, that the meeting was held no earlier than a few weeks prior to that date.

These minutes make clear that no arrangements had yet been made for the Officer-in-Charge, Project Blue Book, US Air Force, to visit Canada. The RCAF appears to have been dragging its feet.

It is also reported that the chairman of the Committee was particularly interested in a recently-published book in which contact was claimed with the occupants of a landed saucer, and that the book's author had actually taken a flight aboard a saucer.[24] The chairman indicated he intended to obtain further information concerning the author's source of information. This type of internal evidence illustrates the seriousness with which the flying saucer matter was regarded.

Smith then presented a report on DOT activities to date, with future plans. This report appears as Annex 5. This report makes clear that there were really only two acceptable alternative explanations for flying saucers —natural electromagnetic causes or alien vehicles, and that it was desirable to get some measured data in addition to the qualitative observations. This was the purpose of establishing the Shirleys Bay station. It was felt that certain of the phenomena would probably be accompanied by physical effects which would be measureable. Thus, the disturbance recorded on August 8, 1954 must have been recognized as a major event and must be registered as such in documents not available to the public.

A further document which has come to my attention is a Canadian government report on Project Blue Book, the US Air Force study of UFOs. This report is also undated but internal evidence makes it clear that it originated in 1952 or 1953. This would therefore appear to be the missing report referred to earlier. It was originally classified SECRET but has now been declassified.

This report notes that there are certain patterns of sightings around major port areas and atomic energy establishments. This pattern has been maintained over succeeding years. Another interesting item is that five percent of the reports came from scientists at the missile launching base at White Sands, New Mexico. This destroys the myth that scientists never see UFOs, as already mentioned in Chapter 3.

This report also refers to a Project Stork at Columbus where scientists assisted Project Blue Book in the breakdown of flying saucer data. In all the UFO literature I have read over these many years, I have never seen reference to this project before so it must have been highly classified.

Most of this report concerns the routine activity of Project Blue Book and it ends with expression of a desire to exchange information between Canada and the USA and that Captain Ruppelt, Officer-in-Charge of the project, be invited to visit Canada.

Many questions remain unanswered. Why was Project Magnet suddenly officially closed down just when a major magnetic disturbance was recorded on the instruments? Were there further meetings of the Project Second Storey Committee? Why was the 1953 Project Magnet report with its startling conclusion not recorded in the Second Storey minutes? These and other questions can only be answered by the federal government and it is not about to do so.

Wilbert Smith continued his work on his own time, as authorized by the government. In 1960 he wrote:

Recent Project Magnet actvities have dealt with following up any and all leads. Many of these leads were dead ends, but a few were quite significant and well worth the overall effort. At the present time a definite pattern is emerging, and the ground-work is being laid for a new technology which may literally lead us to the stars.[25]

There you have the **available** facts of Projects Magnet and Second Storey as recorded in official files made available to me. Much more went on behind the scenes which is still buried in secret government files, which I am unable to document adequately. But here is one example of the sort of thing I refer to. In 1959 Smith was closely involved with the Office of Naval Intelligence, US Navy, and the Central Intelligence Agency (CIA) in the investigation of a situation in the USA in which a certain Mrs. Swan was in mental contact with the occupants of UFOs. This communication manifested through the technique of automatic writing.[26] Proof of this contact was shown when Mrs. Swan's communicator predicted that UFOs would be seen at specified times and places. They were in fact seen by US Intelligence Officers who also made contact with the occupants.

This has the appearance of a wild tale, I realize, but part of it is documented in a "Memorandum for the Record" which has now been released by the US Government and is printed in its entirety in a 1974 book by Robert Emenegger.[27] Only the names of participants have been deleted to protect their identity. This episode is confirmed by Dr. David M. Jacobs in his doctoral dissertation, subsequently published in 1975.[28] Jacobs has researched the US Air Force Project Blue Book files in the Archives at Maxwell Air Force Base, Montgomery, Alabama, but since relocated to the National Archives in Washington, D.C.[29] Through my own sources, I know this story to be true. We are left in the position of being denied the most important aspects of Project Magnet due to government secrecy.

Smith was informed of many things by his contact, who identified himself as AFFA, among these being that this planet is afflicted with areas of reduced "binding". Matter is held together by the equilibrium of all the forces acting within it and the alteration of any of the fields reflects in the binding forces within the matter. As Smith said:

> Not all fields within matter are due to that particular chunk of matter, or even to matter itself, as the field structure within which matter is immersed may be altered by outside influences.

This all means that the binding forces within matter are **not** the fixed and immutable quantities we have believed them to be.

On this earth, and reasonably close to its surface, the field structure is predominantly constant, except for certain regions, and matter displays reasonably stable characteristics throughout the world.

However, there do exist certain regions which may be termed vortices, in which one or more of the fields are different from the values generally prevailing elsewhere. Within these regions there may be substantial changes in the binding forces of matter, depending upon the nature and extent of the field differences.[30]

Smith was informed by his contact that we had means of detecting areas of reduced binding within our technology and that we should build suitable instruments and pay attention to what they registered.

The significance of this reduced binding was that when an aircraft would fly through such an area, if it was not stressed sufficiently well, the aircraft would fall apart. Apparently a number of air crashes could be attributed to this. It would certainly be helpful if such areas could be located so that aircraft could avoid them.

Smith was given the principles of a "binding meter" and he then set out to work out the detailed design. He and his colleagues constructed a number of these instruments and had them tested and many areas of reduced binding were located. One of the problems encountered was in the discovery that these areas tend to move about so that they are not always found in the same spot.

After testing, which proved the validity of his source of information, Smith passed this information on to the Aviation Branch of the Department of Transport for further testing. They failed to do anything about it. As Smith said:

> Unfortunately, because of the unorthodox source of this information, efforts so far to obtain official recognition have resulted only in more letters being added to the "crank file".[31]

Another interesting aspect of Smith's work is that in 1952 he was provided by the US Air Force with a metallic fragment which had been shot from a flying saucer by a jet fighter near Washington, D.C. in July of that year. The fragment was loaned to him for study purposes, but was returned to an authority "much higher than the US Air Force."[32] I have confirmation of this episode from a highly reliable source.

In 1955, Smith told the House of Commons Special Committee on Broadcasting that the results of his UFO measurements were "nil", which contradicts the facts already reported here.[33] It is evident that he was expressing the official government public policy of the time, bearing in mind that he was addressing a Parliamentary Committee as a Public Servant. He continued to publicly express his personal opinions on the matter, which were in agreement with the facts reported in this book.

Shortly before Wilbert Smith passed away, he wrote a small book in which were published some of the basic scientific concepts as revealed to him by our visitors from space, or "the boys from Topside" as he preferred to call them. In this book he said:

> Many shining nuggets of truth lie buried at our feet and if we are not too proud to dig, we will find them . . . Truth is not hidden; it is available to all and is the same for all. Apparent differences must be due to inadequate understanding.[34]

While Smith named his work **The New Science,** it is, of course, new only in the sense that it is new to us; like all other natural laws, it has always been in existence and its truth is as old as Eternity itself. It was typical of Smith's modesty and integrity that he should claim no personal credit for this work and he inscribed his original manuscript with a simple by-line:

> Assembled by W. B. Smith from data obtained from Beings more advanced than we are.

In his book, Smith shows that our universe consists of twelve "dimensions", or four "fabrics" of three parameters each. These twelve parameters are the necessary and sufficient conditions for the existence of the physical universe as we have it, he said. He admitted this sounded rather weird, but insisted "it is quite self-consistent and from it we can obtain rational explanations of all of which we are aware and **entirely without anomalies**". Under these concepts, the velocity of light is **not** a constant and is **not** a limiting velocity. Time is **not** a continuous flow but under varying conditions will show different quantities within specific intervals. Gravitation is **not** a primary force but a function, and is subject to manipulation, he tells us. (Emphasis added).

As the Foreword to his book states:

> A first reading of this book will undoubtedly leave the reader with many questions in mind, and with few answers immediately obtainable. As a work which purports to provide a comprehensive yet simplified understanding of the universe and of reality as we observe it, it will appear most novel in its development, intricate in its ramifications, and will challenge the most vivid imagination. Yet, the implications are far-reaching in their significance and the applications innumerable. The serious reader is advised to read it often, and most important of all—to think.
>
> THE NEW SCIENCE attempts to provide a fundamental understanding of reality in general and of our known universe in particular. It advances a unified concept governing our awareness of reality, explains the generation of this reality, and describes the factors which mold it into the numerous forms in which we find it. To some extent it is not a "first" attempt. For centuries philosophers and scientists have, with varying degrees of success, framed hypotheses with the same considered objective. It may be said that such attempts at a unified understanding of the universe is a natural result of man's inquisitiveness and his searching need of the ultimate order. THE NEW SCIENCE is unique, however, in bringing into play not only those factors which are usually considered as physical or material, but also the more subtle yet no less important influence of the mental and spiritual.
>
> The work was produced after many years of thought and investigation. Existing concepts were considered in all their scope and depth. It is the belief of many that numerous "clues" were obtained from civilizations much more advanced than ours. Some of the more physical aspects were confirmed by actual experiment and the less tangible considerations tested against observable data and evaluated for consistency.

Wilbert Brockhouse Smith passed away, from cancer, on December 27, 1962, at the young age of 52. Canada lost a curious and sincere figure.

CHAPTER 8

THE SCIENTIFIC APPROACH
— POSITIVE or NEGATIVE?

The normal conduct of scientific research involves the use of hypotheses and theories, and those proposed are based upon known physical laws. The simple fact that science is forever learning new facts and discovering new 'laws' is evidence enough that what we know today can be changed by new knowledge gained tomorrow. Why, then, do scientists propose hypotheses based simply on 'known facts' or 'laws'?

It is quite apparent that science fiction writers have a far higher rate of success at prediction of the future than do scientists (disregarding repetitive events) and this is due to their casting aside the chains that bind scientists to known 'principles' and 'laws'.

Take the matter of time, for example. Time presents no problems to the science fiction writers. They have their characters crashing through the 'time barrier' regularly. Yet to the average scientist, the barrier remains as impenetrable as ever. But why? Science cannot tell us the true nature of time. It is one of the least understood matters in science today. All our actual measurements of time are relative to our terrestrial environment and experience. As Dr. Thomas Gold tells us:

> Introspective understanding of the flow of time is basic to all our physics, and yet it is not clear how this idea of time is derived, or what status it ought to have in the description of the physical world . . . It may be that no very profound improvement in our understanding of time will ever take place, but it could also be that some new physical theory will be devised one day that depends on, or defines, a different concept of time . . . our present understanding is inadequate and is perhaps holding us back from a better description of nature.[1]

One of the major obstacles scientists throw in the path of UFO believers is the understanding that the time factor involved in physical travel between solar systems is so great as to make such travel completely out of the question. But if we start afresh and freely admit that we do not in fact understand even the basic nature of time, we cannot then allow time to be a barrier to our thinking. We should adopt the position that time may be something quite different from what we have believed, and may not in fact be an obstacle. Then interstellar travel becomes a definite possibility. As science already admits the probability of intelligent life in other solar systems, then there is no reason why such intelligent beings may not have discovered the way to overcome time as we now think we understand it, i.e., to break the time barrier.

The time barrier—the understanding that the apparent limitation of the speed of light would make interstellar journeys of such long duration as to be out of the question—is the most frequent argument I hear against the possible existence of space visitors in our atmosphere. When we do not have even a basic understanding of time, it cannot be used as a valid argument against interstellar travel. Carl Sagan[2] tells us that relativistic space flight is possible within the lifetime of a space traveller, due to "time-dilation", which is "a kind of metabolic inhibitor but one that works on the entire spacecraft". Such a technique is possible within "known scientific principles". Unfortunately, our relativistic space traveller will return to Earth thousands or millions of years later (Earth time). It is highly unlikely that one generation would consider investing the vast sums of money necessary for such exploration when the results of it could only become known so far in the future. Indeed, Earth civilization may then no longer exist. This form of space travel, then, is not likely ever to be undertaken. Obviously, we need a better method—one which will bring our traveller back within, at the most, the same generation.

The time barrier may not exist in fact. We are led to believe it exists because we have not yet found a way to overcome time. It is what we believe to start with that affects all our thinking, and hence the conclusions we draw, and the hypotheses we propose.

An interesting incident occurred in Chile on April 25, 1977 when a corporal in the Chilean Army, camped out at a post near the border, went to investigate a UFO which landed nearby. He returned fifteen minutes later, unable to recall what had transpired in the interval, but now had a five-day growth of beard (he had been clean shaven) and his digital wristwatch had advanced five days but had stopped at 4:30 a.m. the time he returned to his post.[3] Is this, perhaps, a case of time travel?

UFO believers, so-called, (meaning, for this discussion, those who subscribe to the Extra-Terrestrial Intelligence or ETI hypothesis) are accused of all sorts of things, including ignoring physical laws and 'wanting' to believe in ETI.[4] Let us examine these two accusations.

As for ignoring physical laws, it seems to me to be more correctly a case of recognizing that physical laws are sometimes found to be incorrect or inadequate, as some have indeed proved to be, e.g. the cases of parity and time-reversal invariance.[5] Let us admit that physical laws are merely statements concerning past observations and what can thus be expected in the future, (repetition of similar events under identical conditions). Sometimes new observations require a restatement, or a discarding of a law. Limiting our thinking solely to speculation based on present knowledge can stifle all sorts of discovery, so it is better to unshackle our minds for greater chance of success.

As for the 'will to believe', I think it is more correctly a case of 'willingness to accept' the ETI hypothesis because of the recognition that physical laws may not be as rigid, or all-inclusive, as we are taught they are. But really, this willingness in the positive sense, on the part of many ufologists, is no different than the will **not** to believe or the 'will not to accept' which is the trademark of orthodox science. The will in the negative sense is equally as strong as that in the positive. An important point, usually overlooked, is that most 'believers' were sceptics originally, but only came to believe after careful study of the evidence and drawing a conclusion regarding ETI. These people, which includes myself, are in a different category from those who believed all along, because the latter category includes some who have not based their belief on the available evidence, but simply on psychological or religious desires, etc.

So, as you see, those who accuse 'believers' of committing scientific sins are themselves committing the same sins, only negatively rather than positively. But the 'believers' have the advantage in that they are more receptive to the possibility of finding new knowledge because they have cast off the chains which still bind those on the other side of the fence.

There is no such thing in science as complete impartiality because despite all the controlled conditions of the laboratory, the scientist bases his thinking on present knowledge. As a result, many great discoveries were exactly that—discoveries—but accidental ones, while 'playing about'. This is known as the "method of haphazard experiment", which is simply trying something new to see what happens, without anything specific in mind, that is, without direction. Alexander Fleming said he was "just playing about" when he discovered penicillin. Few great advances have been made by making a great leap to what on the surface may have seemed a completely improbable hypothesis, and then searching for evidence to support it. In retrospect, there is no reason why the great 'accidental discoveries' could not have been made by such a means. It didn't happen because scientists did not stretch their thinking far enough.

The point I am making is simply that the **approach** we take to UFO investigation is of utmost importance, particularly as we have found so little physical evidence in the form of hardware which scientists want for examination in their laboratories. The paucity of hardware is all the more reason to stretch our imaginations to possible causes of the phenomena (which are known to exist) as this can give us new ideas on avenues of research not previously explored. Even thinking in terms of hardware may be causing a large part of the problem of investigation. If ETI has the power or knowledge to control molecular structure, for example, (not beyond possibility) the UFOs we see may be simply temporary constructions (not necessarily metallic) which can be disintegrated into atoms at will, thus leaving no hardware behind.

We can adopt a negative approach and disregard everything that contravenes known physical laws and knowledge, as most scientists have been doing for years, or we can take a more positive approach and stretch our imaginations to the ETI hypothesis (or any other hypothesis you like) and thereby be in a far better position to examine any form of evidence whether it might defy known laws or not, as in that way new laws might be discovered which are unthought of today. I suggest that greater use of the latter approach is more likely to bear fruit in solving the UFO enigma in the long run.

CHAPTER 9

CLUES TO A PARALLEL UNIVERSE

For too long, we have thought of our universe in purely physical or material terms—physical galaxies, stars and planets and physical beings like ourselves. A broad consideration of phenomena which occur make it clear that we need to look beyond the bounds of physical science to explain much of what goes on around us. We live in a far stranger universe than we were taught to accept in our school days. Incredible events take place which, although they appear to be in the realm of science fiction, have nevertheless been documented as factual occurrences. That they do take place must cause us to take another look at our surroundings. In this chapter we will look at evidence which clearly shows that paraphysical, parapsychological or metaphysical events do occur despite the fact most people have not been willing to accept them. We will see classes of events so strange they will seem incredible to those who can accept things only in physical terms.

There are many aspects of our existence in this physical universe which cannot be explained by physical theory or known physical laws. Many strange things happen, either spontaneously or by will, which are in the realm of the paranormal, parapsychological, paraphysical, metaphysical or whatever you like to call it, even though the majority of scientists refuse to accept the evidence. They have not studied the data. It is out of their field.

Parapsychology has been defined as the study of phenomena beyond the present scope of psychology. Paraphysical and metaphysical mean "above or beyond the physical" and paranormal is of course "beyond the normal" so all these terms really mean the same thing.

Because there have been a great many hoaxes in the field of parapsychology is not cause to say that parapsychology has no basis in fact. Hoaxers and charlatans are found in any field, particularly where there is financial profit. Too many reliable and competent investigators have found truth in it for it all to be dismissed with a sweep of the hand.

Science as a body now accepts parapsychology as a serious and legitimate study. Some of the world's great universities grant doctorates for research in this field and work proceeds on a continuous basis. This new science has its own professional organ, **The Journal of Parapsychology**. Psychical research has indeed attained scientific respectability.[1]

In 1882, the Society for Psychical Research was founded at Cambridge University in England under the presidency of Henry Sidgwick, Knightsbridge Professor of Moral Philosophy. During its history, the Society has had the support in its Presidential Chair of such men as Professor Balfour-Stewart, F.R.S.; the Earl of Balfour, O.M.; Professor William James; Sir William Crookes, O.M., F.R.S.; Sir Oliver Lodge, F.R.S.; Professor Charles Richet; Bishop Boyd Carpenter; Professor Henri Bergson; Dr. F.C.S. Schiller; Lord Rayleigh, O.M., F.R.S.; Professor William McDougall; Dr. W. F. Prince and others.[2] We cannot be so naive as to believe that all these scholars were taken in by charlatans. They were acutely aware of the possiblility of hoaxes and hence made every effort to uncover them. After overseeing and conducting every conceivable kind of experiment, they remained convinced of the reality of paranormal phenomena.

The world's first official Laboratory of Parapsychology was set up at Duke University in the USA in 1931 by Dr. William McDougall, one of the most universally-respected psychologists, with the assistance of Dr. J. B. Rhine, who later headed it for many years.[3] The first thing scientifically proved here was that a "psi capacity", a non-material component in life (a soul?) exists. Such a claim was only made after hundreds of thousands of tests were conducted under strict scientifically-controlled conditions.[4] It was also proved that this non-material element was capable of exerting energy against material objects.[5] The Duke experiments also showed that distance (space) was not a barrier to the functioning of extrasensory ability.[6]

Extrasensory perception (ESP) and other psychic matters gained formal scientific recognition in the USA in December 1969 when the Parapsychological Association was admitted to affiliation with the American Association for the Advancement of Science.[7]

Since leaving NASA, the American astronaut, Captain Edgar D. Mitchell, lunar module pilot of Apollo 14, has set up the Institute of Noetic Sciences to further studies of human consciousness including the faculty for ESP. Dr. Mitchell started reading the parapsychological journals and the works of people such as Dr. J. B. Rhine, and, he says, "found much to my surprise that the more I read, the more my skepticism melted away. Experiments of my own . . . so fascinated me that I launched it as a full-time study".[8] Here is an example of how study of the data can radically change a person's attitude to a subject.

For the better part of its four hundred year old history, modern science has been materialistic, mechanistic and anti-spiritual. It has refused to consider any phenomena that could not be weighed, measured, analyzed, and reduced to pat chemical, physical or biological formulae. Not until the establishment of parapsychology as a university study in the second and third decades of this century did modern science grant even a grudging hearing to the few unorthodox spokesmen for the non-material component in life.[9]

At Johns Hopkins University—one of the most staunchly conservative and respected medical institutions—a course in psychic healing and other unconventional treatments is being taught under the guidance of Dr. Lawrence Green, head of Hopkins' Division of Health Education.[10]

In the USA alone, research into parapsychology is being undertaken at the Institute of Noetic Sciences (under former astronaut Edgar Mitchell); the Foundation for Research on the Nature of Man (founded by Dr. J. B. Rhine); the Parapsychology Laboratory of Duke University; the Psychical Research Foundation; the Division of Parapsychology, University of Virginia; the American Society for Psychical Research; the Stanford Research Institute; and Harvard University. Parapsychology is one of the fastest growing fields of academic research in universities today.[11]

The Catholic Church is now showing greatly increased interest in parapsychology and this is reflected in a course being taught at the Vatican's own Lateran University in Rome. This course is taught to theology graduates from around the world and includes levitation, ESP, telepathy and psychokinesis (the power of the mind to exert influence on matter). Dr. Andreas Resch, the church's leading expert on parapsychology is the lecturer, and he keeps in touch with leading researchers around the world to keep up-to-date on current developments in these fields. The work of Dr. Resch is a definite indication that the attitude of the Catholic

Church to parapsychological matters is changing.[12]

Madame David-Neel tells us, after fourteen years in Tibet, that telepathy is a branch of the Tibetan secret lore and seems to play the part that radio has taken in the west. Tibetans assert that telepathy is a science which can be learned like any other science by those who have proper teaching and are fit instruments to put the theory into practice.[13]

Astrology has been a subject of controversy for thousands of years. Today, millions of people accept astrology as fact. Yet the scientific community disputes all claims to truth of the subject. To scientists, believers are simply deluding themselves. However, a study has been made by Michel Gauquelin which puts all the scientific data together, and shows that the marvellously intricate human machinery seems to be sensitive to extremely subtle cosmic influences radiating from the planets close to our Earth.[14] We are told by Dr. Frank A. Brown, Professor of Biology at Northwestern University:

> Man is unquestionably and inextricably linked by many threads with the rest of the universe, not only by way of the physical instruments he has invented and constructed but also by way of the amazing sensitivities of his own living substance.[15]

Nobel Prize-winner in physics, Dr. Gerhard Herzberg, told an international conference in Ottawa on March 2, 1978, that an uninformed and ignorant public is behind the recent rise in popularity of 'pseudo-sciences' such as astrology".[16]

The public in general may possibly be uninformed and ignorant but this does not prove that astrology is not based on fact. I do not think that Michel Gauquelin and Dr. Frank Brown are uninformed and ignorant, yet they tell us there is factual basis to astrology.

"Ether", the magical, living substance that was assumed to extend from the Earth's surface to the stars, was discredited and replaced in the nineteenth century with empty and sterile "outerspace". But throughout the twentieth century science has discovered that "outerspace" (or the "interstellar medium") is not empty but filled with radiation and various fields of force that constantly affect the Earth.[17]

In other words, the ether of the ancients is indeed present, but that is a dirty word to scientists. Call it what you like, it is still ether. There is still a great deal we do not know about these forces and radiations which permeate "space" but they are no doubt the key to all aspects of the paranormal which are discussed in this book. Scientists have begun to accept the idea, until recently unbelievable, that the influences of space penetrate everywhere including the best-protected laboratories, affecting all organisms, even those placed in apparently uniform conditions. In fact, the results show that there are no truly uniform conditions on Earth.[18]

The idea of a mysterious vital force or energy permeating nature, including the human body, is an ancient one that has spread under many names over the centuries. It is the **Prana** of the ancient Hindus, and the **Vis Medicatrix Naturae** of Hippocrates. It has been rediscovered from time to time as the **Mana** of Polynesian primitives, the **Telesma** of Hermes Trismegistus, the **Pneuma** of Gallien, the **Astral Light** of the Kabbalists, the **Spiritus** of Fludd, and the **Magnetic Fluid** of Mesmer.[19]

It has long been believed that clairvoyant persons could see this aura, which is a radiating luminous cloud surrounding the body and that it differed from person to person in colour and character, expressing the health, emotional and spiritual attributes of the subject.

In 1866, the brilliant German scientist Baron Karl von Reichenbach, celebrated for his fine work in chemistry, mineralogy and geology, had published his **Aphorisms** based on hundreds of careful experiments with psychic individuals who could perceive an emanation from magnets, crystals and human beings. He studied the characteristics of this force with great care only to have his findings ridiculed by his dogmatic fellow scientists. He referred to this mysterious force as **Od**.[20]

He found that this force can be demonstrated visually, by heat, and by electric charge, in plants, animals and humans. It is generally blue in colour, and may well be the most important force in the universe. Von Reichenbach believed this force to be the life energy. He claimed it fits between electricity, magnetism and heat, without being identifiable with any of the three. It is, he said, a cosmic force that radiates from star to star and has the whole universe for its field, just like light and heat. He was the first man to make a scientific case for the reality of this force by conducting hundreds of careful experiments, but his painstaking researches were rejected by his fellows. His brilliant record in orthodox scientific fields did not protect him from their wrath.

In 1908, an English physician, Dr. Walter J. Kilner, conceived the idea that the human aura might be made visible if viewed through a suitable substance and he experimented with dicyanin, a remarkable coal-tar dye. Using his viewing screen, many people were enabled to see the aura. Kilner said there were marked changes in the appearance of the aura in differing states of health and that his viewing screen could be used for diagnosis. Many reputable medical men endorsed Kilner's findings, but his work was too unconventional to make much impact on the professional world. Kilner's researches were extended by Oscar Bagnall, who wrote **The Origin and Properties of the Human Aura,** published in 1937.[21]

Those persons who have been able to see the aura are some psychics who can see it unaided, and some ordinary people who can see it with the aid of Kilner screens or aura goggles. These devices do not work for all, however, due apparently to the different ways in which people's vision is affected by use of the devices, just as one prescription lens will not help everyone's vision. It is only fair to say at this time that many clear-thinking and reputable investigators confirm this work and one cannot discount the considerable body of supporting evidence.

Dr. Wilhelm Reich, who called this force **Orgone Energy** in the mid-twentieth century was the latest discoverer of what von Reichenbach called **Od** in the previous century.

Reich built an 'orgone energy accumulator' which accumulated orgone energy from the atmosphere around the human body. This accumulated energy, he claimed, could cure disease. The US Food and Drug Administration claimed that orgone energy did not exist and that Reich's books and scientific literature constituted "misbranding" when associated with his orgone energy accumulator. In other words, the FDA implied that Reich was a "quack" and that the public must be protected. This, despite the fact that other scientists had verified Reich's claims. Yet the FDA never gave Reich's accumulator fair tests.

The books, journals, annals, pamphlets and papers written by Dr. Reich, in thousands of copies, were burned by the US Government between June and August 1956.[22] This was the result of a civil action brought against Reich by the US Food and Drug Administration. The Decree of Injunction handed down by the United States District Court for the District of Maine, Southern Division, on March 19, 1954, ordered his books and papers "destroyed".[23] This is freedom of speech? If you think that political and scientific censorship do not exist in modern Western Society you are urged to read **Wilhelm Reich** (St. Martin's Press) and **Orgone Energy** (Exposition Press) where the full story of Reich's persecution and untimely death is opened to public view. We do not live in a free society despite what you may think. Fortunately Reich's books are now coming back on the market so you had better buy them up now before another order to burn is issued.

Reich died a broken man in Lewisburg Penitentiary, Pennsylvania, on November 3, 1957, at the age of sixty. He refused to stop referring to "orgone" in his books after being ordered to desist by the Food and Drug Administration. He was tried, found guilty and sentenced to prison.[24]

The work of George de la Warr is clearly reported in **New Worlds Beyond the Atom** which includes a photograph of the aura of a flower in full bloom when only the physical seed was photographed. Clearly, the flower grows into the size and form pre-existing in the aura on a level beyond the physical.[25] This type of work is now common and is known as Kirlian photography after a Russian who also did much work in this field.

It seems that there is indeed a mysterious vital force which a handful of courageous scientists have told us about, but which their dogmatic and orthodox fellow scientists, and the US Government, do not want us to know about. It might upset current theories, beliefs and technology.

Although it is common practice to shout "fake" when people demonstrate paranormal powers, the fact remains that the famous psychic Uri Geller who bends spoons and keys from a distance, even over the television waves, has been subjected to intensive scientific testing and has come up "clean". A considerable amount of this testing was carried out at the prestigious Stanford Research Institute, and by Dr. Andrija Puharich who worked with Uri for several years and testifies to his powers. Despite the cries of the skeptics, and suggestions that Dr. Puharich has lost his mental balance, the Government of Canada has sufficient confidence in Puharich's ability and reliability to place him on contract to develop countermeasures against the beaming of radio signals at us by the Russians, which affects our weather.[26] In a personal interview, Dr. Puharich confirmed this activity to me. It seems that Stanford Research Institute respects his ability as well.

Uri Geller is not the only human with paranormal powers. For some unknown reason, such people are on the increase around the world. A thoroughly-documented case of psychic photography is that of Ted Serios who holds a camera to his forehead, presses the shutter lever, and produces clear photos of scenes around the world. If you don't believe it, read the book by Dr. Jule Eisenbud.[27] Serios has been thoroughly investigated and tested under scientifically-controlled conditions.

Cases of psychic healing are becoming legion. Dr. Andrija Puharich also conducted a scientific study of Arigo, a psychic healer in Brazil. He has cured thousands of patients in seconds, including performing major surgery without anesthesia, sterilization or hypnotic suggestion. Again, this is well documented.[28] Many other medical doctors have also verified such occurrences.

The evidence of all these paranormal events is there for all to see and study for themselves. It is orthodox science that has blinded us and shut our minds to anything beyond the physical. Orthodox and dogmatic scientists think that because they are unaware of the reality of such things that they simply are untrue. We have been brainwashed by the scientific establishment to believe only what they tell us. The scientific establishment is usually twenty-five to fifty years behind the science fiction writers and many years behind such courageous men as Puharich, Reich, Kilner, von Reichenbach et al. This is the knowledge which the "common people" were not supposed to acquire. It was committed to writing in the ancient texts, most of which were long since destroyed in the destruction of the world's great libraries such as that at Alexandria, Egypt. Some books do remain intact, however, and are kept secreted away in such places as the Secret Archives of the Vatican where no one but a favoured few have access to them.

From the dawn of history, people have claimed to have left their bodies in various circumstances, to have retained consciousness, and subsequently to have re-entered their bodies. Many said that they possessed another body, a replica or "double" of the physical body. There are numerous descriptions that have been given by persons of high professional standing—medical doctors, clergymen, professors and scientists—whose

88

word cannot be reasonably doubted by any unbiased person.[29]

An out-of-the-body experience (OOBE), sometimes referred to as astral travel or astral projection is defined as an experience whereby the astral or spiritual "double" leaves the physical body and returns.

Dr. Robert Crookall, a distinguished scientist and late Principal Geologist, Her Majesty's Geological Survey, London, spent many years investigating OOBEs in a scientific manner and tells us that there can be no reasonable doubt that genuine out-of-the-body experiences occur.[30] The only area where there can reasonably be lack of agreement is in the hypothesis which explains the phenomenon. For instance, some people claim these experiences are imaginary, or are dreams. However, such hypotheses are really only tenable if not all the facts are considered. It seems that when **all** the evidence is thoroughly weighed, there can be no doubt that an ultraphysical or spiritual body does at times leave the physical and it is the former in which consciousness lies. The Bible itself tells us "There is a natural body; and there is a spiritual body".[31]

Many witnesses have testified to OOBEs on the part of others. On numerous occasions these witnesses have reported a "fog" or "smoke-like vapour" or "cloud of smoke" which left a person's physical body and gradually became a "double" or "exact duplicate" of the physical body on the bed.[32] Sometimes the release of a "double" was a permanent release, ie, death. In others it was temporary. The fact that in some cases there were a number of witnesses establishes that the events were objective rather than subjective in nature. Oliver Fox gives direction as to how this experience may be induced intentionally.[33]

With regard to permanent out-of-the-body experiences, there is a rapidly growing amount of evidence which indicates that this represents life after death. One researcher (Dr. Raymond Moody) has recently written a book outlining his findings.[34] Dr. Elizabeth Kubler-Ross in her foreword to this book tells us:

> It is written by a genuine and honest investigator. It is also corroborated by my own research and by the findings of other very serious-minded scientists, scholars and members of the clergy who have had the courage to investigate in this new field of research in the hope of helping those who need to know, rather than to believe . . . it is evident from his findings that the dying

patient continues to have a conscious awareness of his environment after being pronounced clinically dead.

She goes on to tell us that all of the patients under study had experienced a floating out of their physical bodies and most were aware of another person who helped them in their transition to another plane of existence. It is a difficult area of research because our present-day scientific tools are inadequate for many of these new investigations.

Dr. Moody explains that the persons he has interviewed are functional, well-balanced personalities, yet they do not tell their experiences as they would dreams, but rather as real events which actually happened to them. The patients, he states, were very capable of distinguishing dream and fantasy from reality.[35] He was amazed by the great similarities in the reports, despite the fact they come from people of highly varied religious, social and educational backgrounds.[36] He was so impressed by the great similarities among various reports that he could easily pick out about fifteen separate elements which recur again and again in the mass of narratives.[37]

So many persons have now reported returning from death after being officially pronounced dead by physicians and related their experience, all of which have many similarities, it is difficult to doubt the reality of such experiences, when they have been carefully and thoroughly investigated by competent investigators such as Dr. Moody.

Let's look at a few of the things reported:

> . . . moving very rapidly through a long dark tunnel. After this, he suddenly finds himself outside of his own physical body, but still in the immediate physical environment, and he sees his own body from a distance as though he is a spectator.[38]

> To complicate the fact that he is apparently inaudible to people around him, the person in a spiritual body soon finds that he is also invisible to others.[39]

> . . . they would just walk **through** me.[40]
> . . . this spiritual body is also weightless.[41]
> . . . he can go **through** the door.[42]
> Physical objects present no barrier and movement from one place to another can be extremely rapid, almost instantaneous.[43]

Independent corroboration of some death experiences has been obtained through attending physicians who have been utterly amazed when the person who had been declared clinically dead described in great detail afterwards resuscitation attempts and other things that took place, and words spoken, while he was supposedly dead, claiming to have witnessed and heard all events while outside his physical body.[44] Obviously, cases such as this cannot be delusions on the part of the patient, and Moody confirms that the people he interviewed were not suffering from psychoses.[45]

Many persons who had been "dead" a little longer tell us of travelling up a "tunnel" at tremendous speed and arriving at a beautiful and peaceful land, with trees, grass, buildings and many relatives and friends who had died earlier. They were told to return to their physical bodies and did so with no conscious effort on their own part.

People are most reluctant to tell others of their death experience due to initial rebuffs. Even clergymen, who would be expected to welcome evidence for life after death, sometimes discount these stories. After being persuaded to tell Dr. Moody of their experiences and receiving his assurance that others had similar experiences, they experienced a profound feeling of relief.[46]

Dr. Moody insists that he is not trying to prove that there is life after death, nor does he think that a "proof" of this is presently possible. He is fully aware that what he has done does not constitute a scientific study and he is not under the delusion that he has "proven" there is life after death. He has been continuing his research and expresses amazement at the number of new cases brought to his attention which confirm what he reported in his book. He has now written a second book reporting on these additional cases which also add one or two aspects to after-death experiences.[47] He has also found that other physicians are doing similar research, notably Dr. Elizabeth Kubler-Ross, and her findings are in agreement with his.

Further evidence of life after death comes from a study of fifty people who had a close brush with death. This study was conducted by a cardiologist, Dr. Michael Sabom, at the University of Florida Medical School. He began this study out of skepticism over similar reports, especially those recorded by Dr. Moody. This study confirmed Moody's findings. "I am totally convinced that these experiences are real", said Dr. Sabom.[48] Another study in California has provided suprisingly similar results, where 21 per cent of the patients surveyed reported that they, too, had moved out of their bodies or to another world.

What some modern-day medical researchers are telling us is essentially the same as what is recorded by mystics of old such as Saint Paul, Saint Augustine, Dante and many others. Even Plato recounts similar stories, a particularly interesting one being the experience of a Greek soldier caller ER whose story is very similar to modern day occurrences.[49] The authors of the **Tibetan Book of the Dead** also give death experiences strikingly similar to those recounted by Dr. Moody and others.[50] If the mystics were self-deluded or psychopaths, the world could do with more of them. No doubt some mystics exhibited mental eccentricities, neurosis, etc., but so do some scientists, artists and critics among others. We must not be unfair in our judgments. It could profit all of us to re-read the writings of the mystics with a more open mind, in view of recent findings.

Although the organized body known as "the Church" speaks constantly of eternal life and heaven, it is almost incredible that it knows nothing whatever of that state and place. It could learn a great deal from the studies referred to here.

That there **is** a spiritual component in life and in the individual which can conceivably live on after the death of the physical body has been proved conclusively in the laboratories of science itself, Duke University being the first to do so as mentioned previously. This component is limited by neither distance nor time.[51] Skeptics can no longer deny the evidence from psychical research on the grounds that it had not been shown that there was anything in the human personality capable of overcoming the time/space barrier we call death. Readers are urged to refer to **Immortality: The Scientific Evidence** for the details of the scientific experiments leading to this proof.[52]

We have so far seen that the evidence suggests there are forces operating around us which are not amenable to our present scientific instrumentation, and that one of these forces is probably the "vital force" which sustains all life, that life forms have an aura which may well be a "soul" or its source of animation, and that this "double" is existing on another plane, undetectable under normal circumstances. It appears that this "soul" or "double" departs the physical body at times, in particular at death, and proceeds to continue its existence in another realm, probably what has come to be referred to as "heaven". What we have then, it appears, is another world, or another whole universe, which interpenetrates our physical world and universe, and is normally undetectable, except under exceptional circumstances. We can refer to this other realm as a parallel universe because it apparently occupies the same space as our physical universe. There may, indeed, be several parallel universes occupying the same space, with each existing on different frequencies as yet undetectable by our instruments.

If our "vital force", "soul", or "double" departs into this other realm and can return to the physical body, is it not logical that it could also return long after death of the physical but without returning to it? This may well account for the records of "angels from heaven" which fill religious literature of all denominations the world over.

Neither Scripture, nor modern science can tell us what elements make up angels. Science is only beginning to explore the realm of the unseen. According to the Bible, celestial beings (angels) have differing rank and authority, from archangels to angels, to seraphim and cherubim. If we have rank and authority in this world, who is to say they don't exist in the next?

The common belief that all angels have wings is not supported by Scripture. Angels are evidently able to move about instantaneously thus defying our concept of space and time. The ancients believed that wings were necessary in order to fly and thus endowed all angels with wings.[53]

Dr. Billy Graham, the world-renowned evangelist, is fully convinced that angels do exist and that they provide unseen aid on our behalf. This is not just blind religious belief—he has made an intensive study of the subject and records many cases of angelic assistance in daily affairs of modern man quite apart from those recorded in the Bible. He describes them as God's messengers whose chief business is to carry out His orders in the world.[54] He also states that they are created spirit beings which can appear and disappear at will.[55] They have changed the destiny of men and nations by their visitations and their knowledge of earthly matters exceeds that of men, he tells us.[56] I would consider Graham to be credible because he **has** done a thorough study of the subject, which few, if any, scoffers have done.

It appears that angels represent the forces of "good" according to tradition and Scripture, and such studies as Dr. Graham's. On the other hand, we appear to have another order of beings representing the powers of "evil". Dr. Clifford Wilson, an Australian scholar and recognized archeologist, has gone on record in claiming that there are spiritual powers which defy explanation in materialistic terms, and that black magic, satan worship, contacts and experiences with evil powers are relatively commonplace.[57]

Dr. Wilson, in a further book says the principalities and powers against whom Saint Paul warned, are very active. "Despite the fact that many academics reject the possibility of demonology," he says, "it should be stated that there is much literature on the subject that comes from highly-educated scientists, clergymen and other scholars. There are well-documented records about demons, readily available to those who do research in the subject".[58]

A noted authority on the Devil (Satanology) is the eminent British surgeon-psychiatrist, Dr. Kenneth McAll who acts as a liaison between the medical profession, the International Fraternity of Psychiatrists and the Church on matters of demon possession, Satanism and exorcism. Dr. McAll is convinced that ostensibly innocent pastimes such as fortune telling, ouija boards, tarot cards, white magic, seance experiments and astrology are the door to the realm of Satanism and should be carefully avoided by everyone. He insists there are hundreds of documented cases of individuals who began by innocent dabbling in such things and who became partially controlled or totally possessed by Satan and his demons.[59]

One particularly interesting case of control by evil powers concerns Adolf Hitler. It has now been revealed in a remarkable book, **The Spear of Destiny,** that Hitler was controlled by such forces. This information was being withheld from the world by Sir Winston Churchill who was aware of the true situation. The man who was going to write that book was a certain Dr. Walter Johannes Stein, a Vienna-born scientist and Doctor of Philosophy who, during World War II, acted as confidential advisor to Churchill regarding the mind and motivation of Hitler and the leading members of the Nazi party. Very considerable pressure was brought to bear on Dr. Stein to dissuade him from revealing the truth about Hitler as Churchill did not want the occultism of the Nazi party to be revealed to the general public. Three days after Dr. Stein finally made his decision to write the book, in 1957, he died. The eventual author, Trevor Ravenscroft, was for ten years a very close associate of Dr. Stein and used Dr. Stein's papers for source material. The book gives the ultimate explanation of Hitler's evil genius and ascent to power.[60]

It is drilled into our heads in childhood that stories of fairies are just that—fairy tales. The expression is used in adulthood to refer to any unbelievable story. However, there seems to be some truth to the existence of fairies also, if we are to accept the word of certain scholars who have done extensive research in this field. There is a fine work by the Reverend Robert Kirk of Scotland which dates from 1691 which makes one think again.[61]

In more recent times, Dr. W. Y. Evans-Wentz, M.A., D.Litt., B.Sc., D.Sc., produced a fine scholarly work which records his years of painstaking research. He concluded that fairies do indeed exist, just as the Reverend Kirk did.[62]

Evans-Wentz states that there is often no essential and sometimes no distinguishable difference between fairies and ghosts of the dead, nor between the world of the dead and fairyland.[63]

Nearly everyone disbelieves in the reality of fairies, but how many people have studied the work of people such as Kirk and Evans-Wentz? Certainly no one will accept fairies as real unless they have seen evidence to convince them otherwise. How many school teachers, or parents of young children, are familiar with the work of these scholarly researchers? The reality of fairies should not be scoffed at before studying these works carefully. Other recommended reading includes the work of Geoffrey Hodson,[64] and E.L. Gardner.[65]

Belief in fairies is still very much alive in Great Britain and many educated people claim to have seen fairies, according to Dr. Katharine Briggs, an English researcher. They have given very good accounts of their experience and there is a body of literature on the sightings.[66]

There is a great tendency to claim that things don't exist simply because we cannot see them or because it has not yet been possible to prove that they do exist. This is illogical. For example, picture yourself behind a fence in which there is but one tiny hole. You are anxious to see what is on the other side of the fence, but are unable to climb it, so there is only one alternative—look through the little hole. This hole is small and hence you are unable to obtain a very broad field of vision—you can see only within a limited angle so everything outside that angle is beyond your vision. Now suppose there is a dog behind the fence outside your field of view where you can't see him. You are unaware of his presence. Is it reasonable to say that there is not a dog behind the fence? Certainly not. It is reasonable only to say that you can't see a dog or that there isn't a dog in the area that you can see. Because you can't see a dog doesn't prove there isn't a dog.

This is the way it is with the electromagnetic spectrum. We see through only a small "window" of the entire spectrum of frequencies—the small portion which represents visible light. We normally see only within this portion of the spectrum. But that is not to say that objects cannot exist outside that portion of the spectrum. We simply can't see anything with our eyes. We know there is a great amount of radiation outside this portion of the spectrum but who is to say that **only** radiation exists there? There may be more dogs on the other side of the fence than people realize.

Mysterious forces, of both good and evil, permeate our planet. Dark powers hold the minds of many people, some in high political office. The evil power controlling Adolf Hitler (as well as a long line of Popes, according to Trevor Ravenscroft) has already been mentioned as a prime example. Our environment is far stranger than most people believe.

Some great thinkers of the world of literature were convinced of the reality of other-world beings. Their beliefs were based not on religious grounds or simple lack of knowledge, but on study of the evidence. In addition to Plato, mentioned elsewhere, we have an example in Sir Arthur Conan Doyle who publicly stated his belief in a fairy world.

The world-renowned astronomer and astro-physicist, Professor Fred Hoyle tells us that signals are being received from the future which control the laws of physics as we understand them. He refuses to elaborate on this startling statement "because the issues are technical".[67] Plato pointed out to us that time is not an element in realms beyond the physical. He may well have been right.

Those who have not had first-hand experience with paranormal events are called upon to make up their minds as to the credibility of these things. A convincing point is that those who have had the more profound type of experiences, such as astral projection (OOBEs) for example, no matter in what age, or to what race or creed they have belonged, or in what part of the world they live, tell us the **same** fundamental things. This unanimity of testimony is quite remarkable. How can you explain the similarity in reports from illiterate south sea islanders newly discovered by the white man, and those from points as far apart as China, Europe and Africa if there is no truth to them?

The main problem in understanding our universe is that there are too many specialists telling us what is or what is not so. Most specialists are not knowledgeable in fields outside their own specialty as they have not studied other fields. Physical scientists, for example, tend to look only at the physical universe and ignore everything that doesn't fit into their knowledge and theories. The more narrowly specialized the "expert", the less valuable is his opinion on other matters. One must have a broad understanding of the whole in order to properly understand its parts. This has been proved by the ecologists. There can be no understanding unless a person has a broad background of interests. Marcus Aurelius has been credited with saying "consider the connection of all things in the universe and their relation to one another . . ." Many things in our universe can be understood in quite a different way when considered in relation to everything else, rather than in isolation as the specialists tend to look at things.

We have been so brainwashed in materialism by the scientific establishment and our education system that most people will not accept new breakthrough discoveries which clearly demonstrate the existence of non-material, or spiritual, phenomena. The evidence is there, but even most scientists will not accept it, because they, too, are brainwashed. They are caught up in their own web. Most scientists fear the ridicule of their peers and will not stray from orthodox thinking. They are trapped in what I referred to in my first book as the orthodox barrier.[68]

My concern here has not been with beliefs, however widely held, but with evidence. I have shown some of the work of a wide selection of scientists and medical doctors who certainly would not go on scientific and public record in support of the reality of parapsychological and other extraordinary phenomena if they did not accept the evidence. Scientists frequently debunk such things whether or not they have studied the evidence (ie., whether or not they know what they are talking about) but they definitely do not stick their necks out in support of such things unless they are fully convinced. We have, therefore, reliable authorities who have thoroughly studied the data, telling us that paranormal phenomena and ultraterrestrial life do exist. I suggest we listen to them as they know whereof they speak. It took great courage for them to speak out, expressing views contrary to those of their peers. They do not gain stature in the eyes of their fellows when they support such things, so you may be assured they are convinced of their findings.

On the other hand, there is a group which dedicates itself to the debunking of matters occult and parapsychological as a matter of principle. This group calls itself the Committee for the Scientific Investigation of Claims of the Paranormal and expresses itself through its magazine **The Zetetic.**[69] Its title has recently been changed to **The Skeptical Inquirer.** Although the group professes to be scientific (many of its members **are** scientists) it nevertheless has one purpose in mind—to convince the public that such things as life after death, astral projection, ESP, flying saucers and all related "cults of unreason" are pure nonsense. Rather than investigating to find out if there is truth to the claims, they set out with their minds made up that there is no truth in them, and that belief in them is bad for the public and bad for science, and these things must be debunked. They set out determined to end all such beliefs. This is hardly a scientific approach. This group are the self-appointed guardians of objective thought. The highly unscientific and unfair manner in which they operate was clearly exposed in a lengthy exchange of letters recently.[70]

So we have many scientists who are accepting paranormal events as real occurrences, and many others who will not and loudly debunk them. To whom should the intelligent layman pay attention? Obviously, we should listen to those who investigate objectively with open minds, with no preconceived ideas as to the ultimate truth. Those whose minds are made up before they start are not being scientific and are biased. A true scientist will consider all facts, all possibilities, and will accept the truth whatever it may turn out to be. We have in parapsychology a repetition of Dr. Edward U. Condon who began a study of UFOs on a contract for the US Air Force with his mind made up that they do not exist.

If ultraterrestrial beings do exist, then where is their abode? A hypothesis can be derived from the data that just as our "soul" or "double" exists in the same space as our physical body and extends outwards a short distance forming an aura, the Earth also has a double interpenetrating it and extending outwards through the atmosphere, and it is this area where the ultraterrestrials live, the vibrations of the "soul" or "double" being compatible with those of the Earth's "double". The same would apply to all other heavenly bodies.

In this chapter I have attempted to show that there is a considerable body of evidence in support of this theory of a "parallel universe". The evidence is far too extensive to cover it in any depth in a single chapter, however I have cited a good cross-section of the scholarly literature on the subject. Disregarding most of the popular books on these subjects, which are primarily narratives of strange events without evidence or even citation of sources, there is enough scholarly literature available to convince the loudest scoffers of the reality of these manifestations. All they need do is study it. Most scoffers will not study it, however. It is a case of "don't confuse me with facts—my mind is made up." The authors of the works cited are scholarly, highly-educated persons who have gone about their work in a thoroughly professional manner. They deserve a fair hearing.

Where does this leave us? We now need a new model of the universe—a super universe or omniverse, which contains not only the physical universe in which we live, but also contains in the same space one or more other universes existing in parallel, superimposed on, and interpenetrating our own, which teems with life in many forms and which contains forces still unknown to orthodox science. These are the forces which perform miracles.

A parallel universe with time flowing in the reverse direction has even been proposed in the prestigious scientific journal **Nature.**[71]

Even Dr. J. Allen Hynek, during a think-tank session, states his belief in the **possibility** of other universes with different quantum rules, or rates of vibration. An alternative he offered was that "our space-time continuum could be a cross-section through a universe with many more dimensions".[72]

CHAPTER 10

THE UFO CONNECTION

On many occasions, UFOs have suddenly **appeared** in the sky without apparently having moved into their position, and after being visible for awhile, have **disappeared** as quickly without moving away. Many such sightings have been confirmed by radar. In this process of appearing and disappearing they frequently go through a foggy or hazy phase—a sort of half-way stage between nothing and something, and vice versa, to put it simply.

Now, if you look at an object and it moves **directly** away from you at tremendous speed, it will seem to disappear before your eyes, but the object is seen to diminish in size during the process until there is nothing left to see. Conversely it increases in size just as quickly if the object is approaching you. This is not the case in the sightings we are dealing with here. These sightings do not involve a change in size of the object viewed, hence the object cannot be approaching or moving away as it appears or disappears. Clouds could be the explanation if the sky happens to be cloudy, but again, we are not dealing with such cases. Many instances have occurred in a clear blue sky in daylight.

We know that all things vibrate, at differing frequencies. We can see only things which vibrate within a certain range of the electromagnetic spectrum. But because we only see things which vibrate within this range does not prove that nothing exists outside it, as already discussed in the previous chapter. The limitation is within our physical bodies; that is, in our eyes and brains.

What seems to be happening is that some UFOs emerge into our space/time frame from a space/time frame different from our own. This process can be described as a conversion of energy and change of vibratory rate. When this occurs, the saucer becomes visible and tangible. It is then solid substance in our world until the energy is reconverted and the saucer disappears. It amounts to a process of materialization and dematerialization (mat and de-mat). Just as there is a spectrum of sound and colour, there is also a spectrum of tangibility[1]

Dr. Clifford Wilson tells us that UFOs appear to be craft which are as solid as a rock, or a house, or a car, at the time they are witnessed. They do leave distinct impressions in the ground after landing. However, they apparently can be changed so that their molecular structure materializes and dematerializes in a way we humans cannot yet accomplish. This explains their sudden appearance and disappearance. It is a case of energy conversion.[2] In other words, at least some UFOs could be of extradimensional origin and move through our spatial coordinates at will and can enter and leave our three dimensional world. It could be said that the UFOs travel up and down the vibrational scale as they move from one plane of existence to another.

Sometimes UFOs suddenly become invisible to human eyes while still visible on radar screens. This is because radar has a greater range of "vision" than humans, and when the UFOs alter their vibratory rate, or frequency, beyond human vision, they may still be within the range of radar reception.

Disappearing UFOs can, in a way, be compared to water. It can be frozen solid into ice and it can be heated into steam, which, as it dissipates, becomes invisible. In reducing a solid to a gas, you are not causing that substance to be anything other than it was before; you are merely breaking up and scattering its component parts, thereby giving it different shape and form. Ice and invisible steam are not two different things but the same thing in a different rate of vibration of its parts.

When UFOs shift into the visible portion of the electromagnetic spectrum, they are solid physical objects in our physical dimensions. In the words of scientist Jacques Vallee:

> Most witnesses describe an object that occupies a position in space; moves as time passes; interacts with its environment through thermal effects as well as light absorption and emission; produces turbulence; and, when landed, leaves indentations and burns from which approximate mass and energy figures can be derived. Furthermore, it gives rise to photographic images and magnetic disturbances.[3]

In other words, they are as solid as you or I. In Chapter 8, I suggested that those in control of these machines may have the knowledge to control or manipulate molecular structure, thus changing it from tangible and visible to intangible and invisible. This speculation is not based on watching too many episodes of **Star Trek** but is derived from observation of actual events. The idea itself goes back to before **Star Trek** was even conceived.

Meade Layne dealt with this extensively in his 1957 book.[4]

Many UFOs first appear as a bright red colour, before they go through a series of changes in the proper order of the spectrum— through orange, yellow, green, blue and violet—just as we would pass through a rainbow—and then disappear. This is how they appear to us when they change their frequency in the electromagnetic spectrum. They are at first radiating at a frequency below that of visible light so that they are invisible. As their frequency increases, they pass through the visible spectrum—the hole in the fence mentioned in Chapter 9—then pass on into invisibility again as they move into the ultraviolet range. The implication of this is that some UFOs are normally invisible to us and are seen only by accident or design.[5]

A space scientist with the National Aeronautics and Space Administration (NASA) is convinced that UFO occupants have molecular control of their bodies and craft, which enables them to materialize and dematerialize. As NASA itself has nothing to say on this subject, and applies pressure on its employees not to discuss UFOs, it is obvious that this scientist, Adrian V. Clark, has strong views and the strength of character to express them as he has done in an interesting book.[6]

Dr. Andrija Puharich, the well-known scientist I mentioned previously, accepts completely the reality of ultraterrestrial beings who, with their spacecraft, are normally invisible to us. He outlines his experiences with these beings in a recent book which makes for fascinating reading.[7]

It now seems quite clear that persons with more than average psychic ability can actually see a little beyond the visible spectrum, (that is, beyond what the average person can see) and this may well explain why some persons see UFOs where others do not. The UFO may be just beyond the normal visible part of the spectrum, in the infrared or ultraviolet range, yet still visible to the psychically-gifted person but not to the ordinary person. It is likely that many persons accused of hallucinating have in fact seen what they claimed, while others saw nothing.

Infrared rays, and the next longest waves, microwaves, are in the heat range of the spectrum and many cases are on record where UFOs radiated tremendous heat, severely burning witnesses.

When UFOs disappear, are they really still there? The answer appears to be 'yes', as Trevor James Constable, a very serious and capable researcher, has photographed them in their invisible state by means of infrared photography. There they are, in the infrared range of the electromagnetic spectrum, where they are unseen by the human eye. What is more, some of these UFOs are quite evidently a form of animal life. If this sounds too weird to be true, then I suggest you read Constable's book **The Cosmic Pulse of Life**[8] as well as his earlier work[9] where all the evidence, and the photographic techniques used, are laid out in detail along with a striking series of photographs taken in the invisible (infrared) range. Constable did not work entirely alone either. He had some reputable scientific colleagues, whom he identifies, working with him. If he was perpetrating a hoax, then his scientific colleagues must necessarily be a part of it. His detailed work must not be taken lightly.

Air Chief Marshal Sir Victor Goddard, formerly of the Royal Air Force (RAF), stated in a lecture delivered at Caxton Hall, London, on May 3, 1969, following his involvement in the RAF's investigation into UFOs in the 1950's that if UFOs are paraphysical, they need not necessarily originate in the paraphysical (invisible) realms of some far off planet, but may originate in the invisible realms of our own Planet Earth.[10]

A very large number of contacts with UFOs involve reports of occupants whose physical form varies quite considerably. Sometimes beings are reported on the ground in close association with a landed UFO. Sometimes they enter the UFO after being seen, and take off and disappear. Some of the reports involve huge ape-like creatures; there are small "men" with slanted eyes and very thin lips; there are reports of occupants eight feet tall, and of others very much like us. Many of these reports have come from engineers, lawyers, physicians, clergymen and others of high standing in their community who display no sign of mental aberration. These are people who are unlikely to make such claims if they had not actually had the experiences. They are as reputable as the scientists who discount such claims, perhaps more so. Although some hoaxes are known to have been perpetrated, mostly by students and other individuals seeking a momentary spotlight, clearly hoaxes are not the answer to the UFO phenomenon. "Some of these experiences must be accepted as genuine" states Dr. Clifford Wilson.[11] Wilson concludes that while undoubtedly some people have suffered from hallucinations with regard to UFOs, there are many who have not so suffered and have actually seen them and have been contacted. He also says that persons with more highly developed psychic abilities are more likely to see these beings and their craft, as some can see what others cannot see.[12]

Dr. Jacques Vallee sums up sighting reports of occupants in this way:

> The entities human witnesses report to have seen, heard and touched fall into various biological types. Among them are beings of giant stature, men indistinguishable from us, winged creatures, and various types of monsters. Most of the so-called pilots, however, are dwarfs and form two main groups; (1) dark, hairy beings—identical to the gnomes of medieval theory—with small bright eyes and deep rugged "old" voices; and (2) beings—who answer the description of the sylphs of the Middle Ages or the elves of the fairy-faith—with human complexions, over-sized heads and silvery voices. All the beings have been described with and without breathing apparatus. Beings of various categories have been reported together.[13]

He further states:

> Through the observations of unidentified flying objects, we are concerned with an agency our ancestors knew well and regarded with terror: we are prying into the affairs of the Secret Commonwealth.[14]

He also expresses the view that the human race is being influenced by a powerful force and that it may represent alien intervention.[15]

Leslie Shepard also expressed the suspicion that the occupants of flying saucers may well be another form of fairies.[16]

Another mysterious aspect of the UFO phenomenon is the Men in Black (MIBs) who so often harass UFO witnesses. The strange oriental-looking men in black suits, driving black Cadillacs with **unissued** license plates, frequently appear at one's door within hours of a witness' sighting and often **before they have told anyone about it.** They warn the witnesses to keep their mouths shut about what they saw and frequently, when followed in another car, just disappear, sometimes at the end of a dead end street. Such incidents are no laughing matter as they are well documented and they happen far too frequently for comfort.

An especially interesting case of an MIB who visited an American physician has been well documented by Dr. Berthold E. Schwarz, Consultant Psychiatrist to the Essex County Hospital Center, Cedar Grove, New Jersey.[17] All indications are that this MIB was a robot or android.

We have already established that a tenable theory to account for the many parapsychological or paraphysical events reviewed in the preceding chapter is that there may be one or more parallel universes interpenetrating our known physical universe. Many thoroughly-documented events of a strange character were outlined which can indeed be explained by such a theory.

This same theory can account for the appearing and disappearing UFOs and the disappearing people somehow associated with them. We have then, a definite relationship between UFOs and a host of parapsychological events through the parallel universe theory. This is the UFO connection. If a parallel universe does exist, and considerable evidence points in that direction, then it appears this may be the source of at least some of the UFOs.

The first step for mankind in learning about the UFO is to learn about the true nature of Man and his divine origin. This is the fundamental key. The future of UFO research lies not in the hands of scientists, but of spiritually-minded people whether they be from the regular scientific professions or just plain ordinary people. An expansion of consciousness is required to encompass the fact that spiritual realms do exist peopled with beings as real on their levels as we are on ours.[18]

EPILOGUE

Ashura directed his eyes towards Jon, who was just putting down some of Planet Earth's records, paused, then asked him what conclusions he had reached as a result of his studies.

Jon replied, "scientists of Earth, it seems to me, were not always leaders—in many respects they were followers. In many instances the common people were aware of the existence of certain phenomena and were able to interpret their meaning quite correctly. Earth scientists scoffed because they hadn't seen similar phenomena. The ratio of scientists to the common people was very small indeed, so their chances of seeing or experiencing these phenomena were proportionately small. The general scientific attitude was that if you couldn't examine it or duplicate it in a laboratory, then it didn't exist".

"Yes", said Ashura, "that was materialism at its worst."

"Scientists only recognized the existence of meteors long after many common people had seen them fall from the sky", went on Jon. "The same applied to our spacecraft. Although seen by millions of people the world over, scientists (with only a handful of exceptions) would not accept them for what they obviously were. Extraterrestrial and ultraterrestrial spacecraft did not 'fit in' with the accepted scientific laws and theories and scientists were threatened by the data, so such things had to be scoffed at and ignored. Their laws of physics were considered sacred which in principle is alright provided the true laws are identified. In some cases they were not. A similar situation existed with parapsychological studies. How could they question the very foundations of their own science? Scientists would only build on what they already had but were unwilling to have anyone tear down the foundations already built.

"Their lack of understanding of time created a mental block to scientists on Earth. All their theories were based on this misunderstanding. Similarly, they would not accept the possibility of control of molecular structure, which we learned eons ago. You see, the Earth scientists went about things backwards. They could not accept the fact that we, and others, were actually visiting Earth. Because this was not accepted, they ignored the possibilities of time travel and molecular control and altered frequency rates.

"Had they accepted our presence, and they had sufficient evidence on which to make this acceptance, they then could have asked themselves—'if we are being visited by alien beings, how do they get here and how do some of them become invisible and visible?' They took a negative approach and decided that materialization, dematerialization and time travel were impossible therefore visitors from other solar systems and other dimensions are non-existent.

"So you see, the common people who thought deeply about what they saw and experienced, were aware of truths which were unacceptable to the body of science. Thus, when science did finally recognize the truths, they were following public knowledge, not leading it. They simply confirmed what millions of people already knew. The remainder of the people were those who were blinded by Authority. They only accepted what scientists told them—or what their Church told them—or their government. There were not enough people who thought for themselves.

"For example", Jon went on, "the Earthlings of some 'Western' nations believed they lived in a free democratic society. How deceived they were! Governments were manipulated by other power structures, while being power-structures themselves, the knowledge of the ancients was suppressed including the knowledge of our existence, and citizens were spied upon by government agencies. They were constantly misled by science, government and church. They lived in a 'fools paradise'.

"The sad part of all this is that it wasn't the people as a whole who brought about their destruction—it was the power structures—the relatively few people who formed the power structures of science, finance, government and religion who controlled the world."

"Yes", said Ashura, nodding his head in approval of Jon's accurate appraisal of Earth's folly. "What happened to Planet Earth was inevitable. Technology was out of control because the four types of power structure really had only one main objective—to retain their positions of authority. As a result, technology was directed to wasteful and destructive ends. The opposing sides were so well armed and the struggle for power so great that inevitably someone was bound to push the final button.

"Although many of Earth's people were aware of our existence the truth was never publicly admitted by any of the great power structures, and because the majority of people accepted what they were told by 'the big four', the truth never became accepted.

"You see, my son, there was no point in making our presence known specifically to the world's leaders because we knew that these leaders would suppress the truth. Our existence was even rejected by many on philosophical grounds. Because we did not act as they expected us to act, we couldn't possibly exist! Our actions were not what was expected of us.

"Earthlings had to learn about the existence of many extraterrestrial and ultraterrestrial races the hard way. It had to be part of their learning experience.

"When the radiation has dissipated, and vegetation and animal life begins to evolve again, we will once more put people back on Earth so a new race can try to do a better job than their predecessors."

First Session—Twenty-eighth Parliament
1968-69

THE SENATE OF CANADA

PROCEEDINGS

OF THE

SPECIAL COMMITTEE

ON

SCIENCE POLICY

The Honourable MAURICE LAMONTAGNE, P.C., *Chairman*
The Honourable DONALD CAMERON, *Vice-Chairman*

No. 80

February, 1969

BRIEF
TO
THE SENATE OF CANADA
SPECIAL COMMITTEE ON SCIENCE POLICY
"SCIENCE, SOCIETY & THE UFO"
BY ARTHUR R BRAY
1187 Agincourt Road,
OTTAWA 5, Ontario

SUMMARY OF MAIN CONCLUSIONS AND
RECOMMENDATIONS

Summary of Main Conclusions

Little progress has been made in twenty-one years of official investigations of the UFO phenomena. Despite the fact that most scientists shy away from the subject, there are some prominent ones who insist the problem is vital and urgent and requires thorough study on a wide-spread scale. These few are supported by many thousands of private researchers who give of their own time and money in an effort to find the truth of the matter.

There can be no doubt of the existence of UFOs. The question is—what are they? And this question leads to the next—why are they here or what are they doing?

Man-made objects and known natural phenomena do not explain the truly unidentified objects. This unknown percentage comprises the objects with which I am concerned. The hypothesis which is most suitable at the present time is that at least some UFOs are intelligently-controlled interplanetary space vehicles and the observational evidence supports this. The fact that such a hypothesis may seem unlikely to some does not invalidate it, despite what many scientists say.

Although various scientific investigations have been conducted into this matter over a period of two decades, none of them have succeeded in solving the problem. If UFOs are merely unknown natural phenomena, why has science not been able to discover what these phenomena are? Whether visiting space ships from other worlds, or terrestrial natural phenomena, the mystery remains unsolved. This is so primarily due to the limitations of the investigations conducted, and of the scientists themselves. The orthodox barrier is an obstacle to the advancement of science and a major change in attitude is required in order to cause the collapse of this barrier.

Apart from the scientific aspects, the possibility of UFOs being interplanetary (or interstellar) vehicles should not be rejected on philosophical grounds. The actions of any such intelligent beings should not be judged in relation to our own reasoning.

113

Humanitarian considerations should be the real objective of all scientific advance, otherwise there is no point to scientific inquiry. The advantages, or otherwise, to the human race on Earth, are vital and sufficient reasons to solve the UFO mystery at the earliest possible date. Investigations over a period of twenty-one years have got us nowhere, but the problem persists.

Recommendations

It is recommended:

1. That the Government immediately recognize UFO phenomena as being of major scientific significance and deserving of serious study, in an effort to remove the stigma attached to scientific and public discussion of the matter;
2. That the Government recognize that the UFO mystery has remained unsolved due to inadequate investigations, and not due to the non-existence of unknown objects in our skies;
3. That complete factual information be released in which the public can have confidence, to reduce the confusion and misunderstanding. Such an act will also encourage people to report their sightings for scientific analysis, instead of keeping them to themselves as is more often the case;
4. That Canada take the lead in UFO investigation by establishing a thorough and fully-objective study of the phenomena, not limiting this study to a few narrow scientific fields as has been the case. Many fields of science, technology and the humanities must be included in this study;
5. That this study be supplemented by an attempt to build a new model of the universe, not limited to known physical laws, but which would permit interstellar travel in short time periods. This task requires, first, a recognition by Science of the possibility that existing models could be false. In other words, scientists must knock down their own "orthodox barrier";
6. In conjunction with recommendation 4, and concurrent with it, that Canada strongly encourage other nations to establish similar investigations on the same basis;
7. That further to recommendations 4 and 6, Canada encourage the United Nations Organization to co-ordinate such national investigations and to establish a control or "filter" centre to assimilate sightings and local patterns to deter-

mine global patterns (with the assistance of computers) in order to obtain the overall comprehensive world-wide view of the situation, which may lead to an eventual solution.

SCIENCE, SOCIETY AND THE UFO

Introduction

1. As I am a serving officer in the Canadian Armed Forces, I must first make clear the following points:
   (a) The contents of this brief, and the opinions expressed, are strictly those of the author;
   (b) Such opinions are in no way based upon information gleaned from the Department of National Defence files;
   (c) This brief does not contain any information gleaned from Department of National Defence files; and
   (d) So far as I am aware, the opinions or recommendations do not in any way reflect policy of that Department.
2. In submitting this brief it is my purpose to draw to your attention, for your consideration, certain facts pertaining to the great world-wide mystery of Unidentified Flying Objects, or UFOs, which is a phenomenon of as much concern to thinking Canadians as to the rest of the world.
3. By UFO, I refer specifically to those flying objects which, after thorough investigation, **cannot** be explained as being man-made objects or known natural phenomena; that is, they remain unidentified. The investigation of these phenomena has come to be known as Ufology.
4. The first question I must answer, probably, is why am I bringing this matter before the Senate Committee on Science Policy? In answering, I must first make it clear that this is a matter which has continued, wrongly I think, to remain beyond the grasp of science despite the frequent pronouncements of many scientists that they can explain all UFOs as weather inversions, balloons, ionized particles, astronomical bodies, swamp gas, hallucinations, hoaxes, and a myriad other man-made objects or natural phenomena. A large portion of the public is unwilling to accept these casual and

115

bland explanations that are so frequently offered, as they know they saw something else.

5. As I stated, this is a world-wide problem, so all nations are immersed in this enigma whether they like it or not. As it is my view that all nations need to investigate UFOs properly and thoroughly, I hope that my bringing the matter to your attention can provide some impetus for Canada to do something about it, and thus to encourage other countries to do the same.

6. It is also my view that little progress has been made in twenty-one years of official investigations. If the present approach to investigations continues, such lack of progress could go on indefinitely, or until some scientific body, finally getting frustrated, states "no evidence has been found to prove the existence of UFOs as being other than man-made objects or known natural phenomena, therefore they do not exist". Nevertheless, the UFOs will probably still be there. All attempts so far to ignore them in the hope they would go away, have failed.

7. To fend off the suggestion that I may be an individual with views shared by no one else, particularly by no one with a high status in the scientific field, I shall quote only four eminent scientists (I could quote others):

    (a) **Dr. James E. McDonald**, Senior Physicist, Institute of Atmospheric Physics, and Professor, Department of Meteorology, University of Arizona:

    "It has become my conviction that the problem of the unidentified flying objects, is, indeed, the greatest scientific problem of our time."[1]

    He stated further:

    "The possibility that the Earth might be under surveillance by some high civilization in command of a technology far beyond ours must not be overlooked."[2]

    (b) **Dr. J. Allen Hynek**, Professor of Astronomy, Northwestern University, and Scientific Consultant on UFOs to the U.S. Air Force:

    "Enough questions exist on UFOs that serious scientific study is called for."[3]

    (c) **Dr. Felix Zigel** of the Moscow Aviation Institute, and a top-ranking member of the Soviet Commission for investigating UFOs:

"The possibility that UFOs are from another planet merits serious consideration." Dr. Zigel released recent sightings of giant UFOs made from the Russian Astronomical observatory at Kazan, which astronomers said were crescent-shaped and they estimated them to be 1600 feet in diameter.[4]

He also stated:

"We must work calmly and thoroughly, employing all the means of modern science. The UFO phenomenon is a challenge to mankind. It is the duty of scientists to take up this challenge to disclose the nature of the UFO, and to establish the scientific truth."[5]

(d) **Dr. James A. Harder**, Associate Professor of Civil Engineering, University of California at Berkeley:

"In the UFO phenomena, we have demonstrations of scientific secrets we do not know ourselves. It would be a mistake, it seems to me, to ignore their existence."[6]

8. Statements of this nature are directly opposed to the views expressed by Sir Bernard Lovell who stated: "I am always surprised by the great amount of discussion which goes on in North America concerning these objects. They do not concern science, but science fiction. Scientists have been able to explain every UFO they investigated. Any suggestion that UFOs are visitors from outer space is nonsense."[7]

9. Clearly, Sir Bernard does not have the complete backing of the scientific fraternity.

10. It is because I am convinced that the solving of this mystery could be of immense importance to the human race, and that a new approach to investigating the phenomena is urgently needed, that I submit this brief.

THE REALITY OF UFOS

11. The question which is probably the most frequently asked is—do UFOs really exist? Certainly they exist. A steadily increasing number of thinking people are becoming aware of the fact that there is much more to the UFO mystery than we are led to believe by those who are in a position to influence public opinion, which includes not only scientists,

but the press, and governments as well. There are too many people in these groups who will go along with a UFO story as long as the bounds of imagination are not stretched beyond what they consider to be a tolerable limit. In the case of scientists, the tolerable limit is usually the present laws of physics. In the case of governments, they accept what Science says is so, or is not so. A tendency of the press is to embellish UFO stories with amusing headlines and personal comments of the reporter in an attempt to cast an aura of illusion on the whole business. Thousands of responsible citizens **know** UFOs exist as they saw them and no amount of whitewash and ridicule can change this. It merely shuts them up. A 1966 Gallup Poll revealed that 5,000,000 American adults have seen UFOs. Of those, over 99.5% failed to report the phenomena to the U.S. Air Force.

12.   It is sometimes stated how strange it is that scientists never see UFOs. Let me assure you that some have.[8] Those who do witness unusual phenomena frequently display a consciousness of colleague criticism that dampens any spirit of inquiry. A UFO researcher in the U.S.A. once sent a questionnaire to one hundred astronomers, in which he asked if they had ever seen a UFO through an astronomical telescope. All replied in the negative. Strangely enough, the same astronomers replied also to a further question that they had never seen an airliner through a telescope either.

13.   A recent case in Canada (in October, 1967) occurred off the Coast of Nova Scotia, when a UFO was seen to settle down from the sky and disappear into the sea. This object was real enough for the Navy to conduct an underwater search for several days. The failure to locate it does not mean the object never existed. This sort of thing simply proves the objects are elusive, not illusions.

14.   A majority of recorded sightings are made by reliable, stable and educated citizens and the most articulate reports come from obviously intelligent observers.[9] These include airline and military pilots, air traffic controllers, radar operators, police and many others. These are people whose jobs depend upon what they see. There are, indeed, photographs verified by top photo laboratories as being authentic, which prove the existence of physical objects. Radar has confirmed visual sightings; Electromagnetic effects have oc-

curred at the time of sightings and in the immediate vicinity; various physiological effects have often been registered, and ground effects of varying nature such as burns, holes in the ground, flattened grass, etc. have occurred. The intensity of radiation measurements has often been found to be much higher after the departure of a UFO, and various effects on foliage have resulted. Several patterns in their behaviour have been recognized.

15. All these forms of evidence testify to the simple fact that UFOs do exist. There is no longer any question about this. One substantial sighting alone, properly verified, proves that UFOs exist. Ten thousand sightings don't prove it any further. As William James wisely said, it takes only one white crow to prove that all crows are **not** black. It is not necessary to possess a UFO and examine it in a scientific laboratory to prove its existence. We all know the sun exists, but man has never touched it, and never will. We measure its effects, visually and in many other ways. Science is asking an already-answered question. The real question that requires an answer at this stage is—what are they? This is the $64 question.

16. To answer this question, the most acceptable scientific thing to do would be to make observations and then propose a hypothesis which is capable of explaining the observed facts—**all** the observed facts. Then continued observations must be made to determine whether the observed facts are still consistent with the hypothesis. If so, the hypothesis remains a valid one. If not, a more suitable hypothesis must be found. It was Sir James Jeans who said:

    "One phenomenon is enough to disprove a hypothesis but a million million do not suffice to prove it."

17. Hypotheses have been proposed by some scientists in an effort to explain UFOs (examples cited earlier) but although some sightings of strange phenomena can indeed be explained by each of these, there still remains an **unknown** percentage which **cannot** be so explained. Those hypotheses, therefore, are not valid as explanations of these remaining unidentified objects.

18. To quote Dr. McDonald again:

    ". . . my position is that UFOs are entirely real and we do

not know what they are because we have laughed them out of Court. The possibility that these are extraterrestrial devices, that we are dealing with surveillance from some advanced technology, is a possibility I take very seriously."[10]

AN ACCEPTABLE HYPOTHESIS

19. A hypothesis has been proposed by many laymen, and a small number of open-minded thinking scientists now accept it as a valid one, and that is that at least some UFOs are intelligently-controlled interplanetary space vehicles. This is known in some scientific circles as the "ETI hypothesis" (extra-terrestrial intelligence). All the observational evidence pertaining to sightings of true UFOs supports this hypothesis as long as we do not limit our thinking by restricting it to only **known** physical laws.

20. An outstanding example of a scientist who openly accepts this hypothesis is Dr. James E. McDonald of the University of Arizona, whom I quoted earlier (para. 18). He has presented briefs on the subject to important groups in the U.S.A. and has expressed utter dismay at the lack of interest in this matter which his colleagues in the scientific fraternity display. An AP report from Washington on July 30, 1968, revealed that he informed the U.S. House of Representatives Science & Astronautics Committee the previous day that the massive power black-out of 1965, and other power failures, may be related to UFOs, due to the numerous instances of these objects hovering near power plants, particularly at the moment of power interruptions.[11] Here we have another pattern being developed, which should be watched closely.

21. Hundreds of cases are on record where automobile engines have stopped upon the near approach of a UFO. Airliners cramped with scores of passengers have been paced at close range and some near collisions have resulted. Human beings have received burns from being too close to these objects. Medical records testify to these burns. Radio & T.V. are frequently cut off during close approaches of UFOs. Much evidence exists that UFOs have in fact landed on numerous occasions, and indentations have been left in the soil, grass flattened, and foliage broken or burned. High

120

ranking officers in armed services around the world have reported encounters with these objects.

22. Not one **known** fact has **disproved** that interplanetary hypothesis despite current acceptance of so-called known "physical laws". Our present laws of physics have never been **proved**. They simply have not yet been disproved. They are valid only so long as all observed phenomena conform to these laws. Using Sir James Jeans as my guide, it is apparent that one phenomenon can disprove something. If therefore, we discover a phenomenon which does not obey the laws of physics, we must not ignore it, in hopes it will go away (as Science has been doing with UFOs for twenty years)—we must take another look at our physical laws.

23. The tendency, unfortunately, is for Science to be dogmatic and insist that nothing can exist which disobeys physical laws. Yet, Science, paradoxically, readily admits there is much we do not yet understand about our physical universe. If we discover something new today, it proves very simply that there was something we didn't know yesterday. As new discoveries are being made daily, there is obviously a great deal we don't know. Perhaps we are still ignorant of much about us because our physical laws are too restrictive and limited. As long as Science insists on compliance with manmade laws, we may never come to understand the true physical laws established during the birth and formation of this vast universe. What Science calls laws are, more correctly, what Science **considers** to be laws based on observations to date. It is a fact, which scientists do not like to have discussed publicly, that some physical laws have been violated in the recent past, and these laws "fell", to use scientific jargon. Three examples which I used in my book are, the laws of conservation of parity, charge conjugation invariance, and time reversal invariance, all of which "fell" within a seven-year period ending in 1964.[12]

24. Scientists believed in these laws because they lacked certain knowledge. They too readily believe that because all evidence indicates a certain thing to be so, all evidence in the future will support this.

25. The fall of parity in 1957 shook the scientific community severely—possibly more than it had ever been shaken be-

fore. My point is simple—it **can** happen again. It **did** happen again.

26. An attitude I am frequently faced with in my discussions on UFO research is that laws of physics are supposedly sacred, and no hypothesis could possibly be acceptable if any part of it requires a contravention of physical laws. This attitude is inherent in our educational system and it is no wonder scientists have this attitude. They are educated to believe these laws are sacred. The fact that several of these same laws have recently fallen does not seem to cause them to be more watchful and ready to accept the possibility of more laws falling. These tremendously important events should have opened scientists' minds to any possibility, but apparently our institutionalized educational system has so indoctrinated them that past failures are soon forgotten. The dogma lingers on.

27. A question frequently posed is—what proof do we have for our hypothesis? When a lack of proof is demonstrated, the questioner immediately rejects the hypothesis. This is not scientific. The proof can yet come. Dr. Herbert Friedman, professor of physics at the University of Maryland, stated that the "hypothetical neutron star is a purely theoretical concept and no evidence for its existence has ever been obtained."[13]

28. Let me state at this point that I am quite familiar with the standard reasons as to why the validity of this interplanetary hypothesis seems very remote. For example, our solar system does not appear to contain any planets suitable for life as **we know it**. But why must any alien life, even superior to us, necessarily be as **we know it**? Dr. S.A. Bowhill of the University of Illinois tells us that the chemistry of our upper atmosphere (above 164,000 ft.) is little understood, despite the many rocket probes we launch.[14] So, if we know so little about our own upper atmosphere, it is fairly certain that we know even less about that of other planets, and far less yet about the lower atmospheres of other planets. Also, papers have been written on the great difficulties we should expect in interstellar travel, but these are all based upon present-day scientific knowledge (existing physical laws) and technology. They are also based upon the "foreseeable" future, and Edward Purcell of Harvard is an example of one who

has tried to demolish such hopes in a devastating manner.[15] To say that UFOs cannot be space ships because of physical limitations is no argument. It is like saying the Egyptians could not have built the pyramids. Even though engineers today admit they cannot duplicate them, they **were** built. If extraterrestrial races are so highly advanced over us, and be capable of feats so advanced that we are not yet able to foresee them because our scientific foresight is based entirely on **known** physical laws. It was Dr. Clyde Tombaugh, discoverer of the planet Pluto, who said:

"It is absolutely impossible for us on earth, with a technology barely a couple of centuries old, to visualize a technology 50,000 years ahead of ours. They would have discovered power sources, laws of physics, chemistry and medicine which in our present state, are simply impossible for us to imagine."[16]

By admitting the possibility of yet unknown laws, the shackles of our present thinking are immediately loosened.

29. UFO witnesses among the general public are accused by scientists of jumping to the unwarranted conclusion that their sightings were of space vehicles or the so-called "flying saucers". However, apart from a few "cultists", the public does not react this way to sightings. The normal first reaction is that they saw an airplane, a balloon, a satellite, a flashing light on an emergency vehicle, or some such conventional object. Only when the witness realizes, after more careful observation, that there was action or performance in a manner which readily ruled out such simple explanations does he go further in his hypotheses. The space ship hypothesis is usually his last. This tendency to take a simple guess first, and then upgrade it when the simple ones are ruled out is characteristic of witnesses and is what Dr. Hynek refers to as "escalation of hypotheses". Witnesses do in fact use scientific method (instinctively, if you like) in arriving at their space ship hypothesis. It is only when they have ruled out, in their own minds, conventional explanations, that they turn to the space ship explanation.

30. Professor Frank B. Salisbury, professor of exobiology at Colorado State University published an article in **Science** in which he stated that we must concern ourselves with the

123

possibility of technological civilization on Mars. Certain peculiarities of Mars and its moons, Phobos and Deimos, he wrote, "are most easily understood on the assumption that they are the product of intelligent beings." Professor Salisbury's views are shared by Dr. Carl Sagan of Harvard University and the Smithsonian Astrophysical Observatory.[17] Similarly, attributes of UFOs are most easily understood on the assumption that they also are products of intelligent beings.

31. The recognition and acceptance of the hypothesis I have been discussing, as a valid one, is the first giant step towards the ultimate solution of this mystery. Indeed, more than one hypothesis can be used at the same time, but as long as this one is ignored, no progress is made. Twenty-one years of official investigations support this statement.

PAST & PRESENT INVESTIGATIONS AND THEIR LIMITATIONS

32. In the U.S.A., the U.S. Air Force has been the official investigating body since December 30, 1947. Their program is currently labelled "PROJECT BLUEBOOK", and was formerly identified as PROJECT SIGN and PROJECT GRUDGE. Little has come from this project of a constructive nature. Periodically, a report is issued to the public on results of investigations to date, and these results are tabulated showing the percentage of sightings identified, after investigation, as specific man-made objects or natural phenomena. The percentage remaining in the unidentified category fluctuates in the general area of 2 or 3 percent. It happens that only about 12,000 UFO sightings have been reported through official channels to the U.S. Air Force in twenty years, yet 5,000,000 Americans have seen UFOs according to a 1966 Gallup Poll, as stated earlier. Further, certain North American space surveillance radar systems are not programmed to record "anomalous observational phenomena". In the words of Dr. Robert M.L. Baker, in his testimony before the Committee on Science and Astronautics, U.S. House of Representatives, July 29, 1968:

"Apparently what is now happening is that the Air Force surveillance radar is throwing away the data that is of relevance for this inquiry. In other words, if it sees something that is not on a ballistic trajectory or not in orbit, it ignores it, it throws it in the garbage. Well, that garbage is just the area of our interest."[18]

33. By the USAF's own admission, their figures do not include reports by letter directly from civilians, at least in some cases. For example, for the period June to September, 1952, 800 such reports were omitted from their statistics released to the public.[19] It is the BLUEBOOK Reports which probably have the greatest impact on public and official thinking in this regard. For example, it has been made clear to me by the Department of National Defence that that Department has been considerably influenced by these reports. It is of particular interest to note that the U.S. Air Force Scientific Advisory Board Ad Hoc Committee to Review Project BLUEBOOK stated at a hearing by the Committeee on Armed Services of the House of Representatives on April 5, 1966, that

"some of the case records that the committee looked at that were listed as "identified" were sightings where the evidence collected was too meagre or too indefinite to permit positive listing in the identified category."[20]

34. It is also of significance that the USAF regularly claims that it "does not withhold or censor any information pertaining to this unclassified program", yet the PROJECT GRUDGE and BLUEBOOK reports No. 1 to No. 12 covering a period from 1951 to 1953 were in fact classified and were only released to the public in 1968 after "persuasion" by the Foreign Operations and Government Information Sub-Committee of the House Committee on Government Operations. These reports contain valuable data as well as important background information on research techniques, and yet they were withheld from the public for fifteen years.

35. The foregoing are two examples which serve to prove that the public in general, and official bodies which place faith in PROJECT BLUEBOOK, are not being correctly informed of all the facts.

Dr. James E. McDonald stated:

"Scientists throughout the world have tended to ignore the UFOs as if they were just so much nonsense. From talking to fellow scientists here and abroad, I have seen that most of them have believed that Air Force Project Bluebook was really studying the UFOs with scientific competence. The trouble was that almost none of these scientists took time off to check for themselves. I did. What I have found is nothing short of alarming. Bluebook and its consultants have simply swept under a rug of ridicule and innuendo thousands of sightings from credible witnesses, sightings of objects that are neither swamp gas nor secret test devices, nor fireballs nor ball lightning."[21]

36. On November 1, 1966, the USAF awarded a contract to the University of Colorado for the conduct of a full and supposedly objective scientific inquiry into the matter of UFOs. The report of this committee was made public early in January this year. This particular project experienced serious internal disruption which cast a cloud of suspicion over the manner in which it was directed.[22] This internal strife resulted in the dismissal of two key scientists of the project. One of these, Norman E. Levine maintains that a lot of evidence points toward the extraterrestrial origin of UFOs, and says that, "If you ignore the extraterrestrial hypothesis, you are ignoring the most significant part of the problem."[23]

37. Let us not be misled by the report of the Condon Committee at the University of Colorado. I predicted in 1967 that the question of what UFOs really are would still remain open upon the publication of this report, as it was highly unlikely that the Condon Committee could present proof that UFOs are space vehicles as Condon's approach has tended to ridicule such a hypothesis and he made public statements to this effect, during the course of the investigation. Further, sighting reports evaluated, many of which have been available to the public through one means or another, cannot disprove such a hypothesis. It is particularly noteworthy that Condon did not **prove** that UFOs are something **else**, and **name** it, so he was forced to leave the problem unsolved. Many sightings remain unidentified, so nothing has really changed as a result of the Condon Report. He has generalized and stated that UFOs are many different things, but has left many well-documented cases unidentified. Indeed, the report was not unanimous by all the committee members, but Condon eliminated this problem by terminating

the services of the dissenters. A shrewd move, to say the least. One of the dissenting scientists has just published a book to bring to official and public notice the discrepancies of the Condon investigation and to point out that much significant evidence was overlooked or rejected.[24]

38. I therefore strongly urge that caution be used in the interpretation of the Condon Report. Let us not be lulled into a false impression that Condon has proved that UFOs are not space vehicles as such proof has not been presented. In fact he did not make this claim. Let us not be fooled into thinking the whole matter is finished, as the question in fact remains open. Its remaining open proved only one thing— that the Committee did not solve the problem. We are left where we were **twenty-one years ago** and my contention that scientific investigations to date have been inadequate to the task has been supported.

39. Many questions can be asked now that the Condon Report has been released. A few of these questions, with answers contained in the Report are listed separately as Appendix "A" to this brief. These answers are very enlightening as to the real findings of the study.

40. In Canada, even less progress has been made to date. In the early 1950s, a study was conducted by an engineer in the Department of Transport. This was primarily a spare time project on the part of the engineer-in-charge, Mr. Wilbert B. Smith, but the Broadcast and Measurements Section of the Telecommunications Division was given the directive to go ahead with this work with whatever assistance could be obtained informally from outside sources such as Defence Research Board and National Research Council. This study was named PROJECT MAGNET. In the final paragraph of his report, Mr. Smith stated:

"It appears then, that we are faced with a substantial probability of the real existence of extra-terrestrial vehicles, regardless of whether or not they fit into our scheme of things. Such vehicles of necessity must use a technology considerably in advance of what we have. It is therefore submitted that the next step in this investigation should be a substantial effort towards the acquisition of as much as possible of this technology, which would without doubt be of great value to us."[25]

41. Since then, little has been done in Canada except to investigate a minor percentage of those reports reaching the government officially. There has been little or no policy direction concerning the study of this matter in Canada, and responsibility has been bounced from one department to another, with individual departments displaying interest only in so far as each department has a particular area of activity. I support this statement by the fact that my personal correspondence with high levels of government, including the former Prime Minister, always resulted in departmental replies clearly showing interest was limited to only one aspect of the problem. For example, Department of Mines and Technical Surveys (as it was known at that time) expressed a view related only to the astronomical aspect. My opinion about the interest of the Department of National Defence was confirmed when it was made clear to me recently that their prime interest was in whether any threat to national security was involved. It having been established that no such threat exists, D.N.D. then passed the task to the National Research Council, which now carrries the ball. No public funds are provided specifically for this purpose and therefore any investigations are limited to what can be accomplished by using funds allotted basically for other purposes, and no staff is allowed for. This investigating responsibility is carried by Dr. Peter M. Millman, Head, Upper Atmosphere Research Section. No matter how capable the project chief may be, he cannot conduct any adequate, comprehensive and thorough investigation of the **total** problem without staff and without funds. NRC cannot even analyze all sightings in Canada over the past twenty years in search of patterns, without people to do the work. They also lack the files from which to work. It is worthy of note, however, that N.R.C. is apparently continuing its very limited activity in this field despite the Condon Report. This, at least, is an indication of clear thinking on the part of someone.

42. At no time, evidently, has there been any one office with an overall interest in all the many aspects of the problem, with the objective of solving the **total** problem, not simply parts

of it, or individual sightings, which leaves the overall matter still a mystery.

43. Late in 1967, considerable publicity was attached to an announcement by the University of Toronto, that a UFO study was being commenced, under the direction of Dr. Gordon Patterson of the Institute for Aerospace Studies. The public has not been well informed of activity of this group, other than an opening forum which conveyed the impression of being a mere attention-getter. In October, 1968, the press reported that this study was on the verge of collapse "owing to a lack of something to investigate, and if some good flying saucer cases don't soon crop up the Institute will have little chance of receiving a National Research Council grant for more costly and intensive study."[26]

44. We have, here, the same old problem. A new study gets under way and they start out only at that point in time, ignoring the many thousands of cases already documented, which could be studied in a search for patterns. The new cases arising could be added to the existing data—they should not comprise the sole data. By ignoring the past records, twenty years of research by others is being overlooked. Do the people of the Aerospace Institute consider themselves the only competent investigators so that they may ignore the work of others? Surely this is not the way to conduct scientific research. Also, I suggest that the sightings reported to the Institute comprise only a small percentage of total observations in Canada during the period, partly due to the fact that few people are aware of the existence of this project. Even those who are aware seem unable to get information from them as to their activities. I have tried and failed.

45. The Science Council of Canada appears to be either completely disinterested in this vital scientific problem, or else it is unwilling to communicate with the public concerning it. I wrote to the Council concerning the matter of UFOs on September 7, 1968 and am still awaiting a reply, despite having hastened a reply by both letter and telephone. Also, the subject of UFOs was conspicuous by its absence from the report of the Science Council, titled A SPACE PROGRAM FOR CANADA, dated July, 1967.

46. Even our Members of Parliament are unable to obtain satisfactory answers to their questions in the House of Commons. Questions have been asked frequently over the past few years and my files contain the pertinent extracts from Hansard. The most glaring example of a brush-off to such a legitimate question by an elected representative of the Canadian public contains the clear suggestion that possible future sightings around Christmas time might be attributed to Santa and his reindeer.[27]

47. The situation is much the same throughout the world, except for Russia where an intensive study has recently been instituted by the Academy of Science and is titled "The UFO Section of the All-Union Cosmonautics Committee" but more commonly known as "The Russian Commission".[28] Dr. Felix Zigel, whom I quoted earlier, is a top-ranking member of this Commission.

48. One of the main difficulties in solving the UFO Mystery is the limited approach to the problem which science has so far taken. There are many limitations to science, and scientists themselves have limitations, many of which I have outlined in some detail in Chapter IX of my book. Scientists themselves have acknowledged these limitations and therefore are not in a position to dispute them. Because of these limitations, many aspects of the UFO problem have not been considered by scientific inquiries. There has been a definite tendency to limit the study to a few fields, primarily astronomy, physics, psychology and meteorology, and in general, each scientist interprets UFO phenomena in terms of his own specialized knowledge and experience.

49. The field is much broader than this, however, and a comprehensive view of the entire problem cannot be acquired without the inclusion of many other fields of study at the same time and with consideration given to the interrelationships and overlaps among all fields. Some other subjects which are a definite part of the overall study are: aeronautics, astronautics, cosmology, evolution, biology and exobiology, history, philosophy, and scientific method (methodology). No UFO study can be completely objective and thorough without the inclusion of all these fields, as I clearly show in my book.

50. With respect to scientific method, I can illustrate the inconsistencies that arise by the following example:

"Until about four centuries ago, it was thought that the sun revolved around the earth, and this was a firm belief because of the sun's apparent movement through the sky. A very satisfactory system of celestial mechanics was developed on this assumption which permitted highly successful prediction of heavenly phenomena. As there is no motion felt of the earth through space, our sixteenth century forebears can hardly be blamed for their views. However, let it be borne in mind that no physical experiment has ever proved that the earth actually is in motion."[29]

51. That is a good example of the inconsistency of scientists— they tell us that scientific method must be employed, that unless a hypothesis can be tested, it cannot be proved to be true. The foregoing example, it seems, cannot be proved by any experiments. Everyone agrees today that the hypothesis is true, and no one argues it. But the fact remains that it has not been proved and is evidently not capable of being tested. If scientists can accept one hypothesis as being true without being able to prove it, why not accept another? At present, we do not understand the conditions under which UFOs appear, therefore a desire that ufology duplicate the methods of other sciences is unreasonable.

52. My book contains many examples which clearly demonstrate that Science, as such, has been inadequate to the task of solving the UFO problem, under present conditions within Science itself.

53. There exists in modern science what I choose to refer to as the 'orthodox barrier'. This barrier is one which excludes unorthodox thought, particularly when manifested in the printed word. To be recognized, one must generally conform to orthodox teachings, orthodox theories and orthodox methods. To penetrate this barrier is a formidable task. The sound barrier, the heat barrier and the escape-from-earth barrier represented physical limitations, all of which have been overcome by science and technology. But the orthodox barrier is a mental barrier which requires only an opening of men's minds to release preconceived ideas which result in narrow thinking.

131

54. Dr. David Green gives his own case as an example of being unable to "reach the establishment", or as I call it, penetrate the orthodox barrier. In **Scientific Research** he describes his work at the Institute for Enzyme Research at the University of Wisconsin where his team developed a new concept of membrane structure and function in mitochondria—a concept that will revolutionize thought on the whole subject of how chemical energy can actually perform physical work in the cell. "But the scientific establishment has ignored us", he states, "It is amazing how difficult it is to reach the establishment. After all, I, too, have position and authority—still it is impossible. I have been fighting them for years. I could write a book about it", he says.[30] I hope he does.

55. It appears to me that so long as a scientist is adding bricks to what has already been built, his work is recognized. But if his new construction requires the tearing down of what was built before, he is ignored. He cannot then penetrate the barrier. This indicates the unwillingness of scientists to admit that what has already been accomplished could be wrong.

56. A change in attitude is required, and when this is brought about, the orthodox barrier need not be penetrated—it will collapse from within.

PHILOSOPHY OF THE PRESENCE OF UFOs

57. Many people reject, on philosophical grounds, the possibility of UFOs being machines controlled by visiting alien races, so we must examine this area of the problem also.

58. Using our present hypothesis, as UFOs have been around for so long, it is frequently stated that if UFOs were visitors from outer space, they would no doubt have landed and made public and official contact with us long before now. But we must consider possible motives for such action, or lack of it. If such a race, or races, is visiting our planet, it may not be their intention to make direct contact with us. A race so highly evolved as they could be, may simply be observing us, as scientists observe the behaviour of animals and insects. It is the same old failing we humans have—extraterrestrial life must be life as **we know it**; physical laws must be

only those laws which **we** have discovered; alien races must travel through space the way **we** would travel through space; and worst of all, they must **think** the way we think. I can only add, that if they do, then God help them.

59. They could be simply observing us on a long-term basis to determine our progress scientifically and morally. We could be considered a source of danger to near-by planets, through the transmission of disease germs and by our detonation of nuclear bombs. To them, we may be as close as next door neighbours, but we would be uneasy if our neighbour on earth detonated dynamite on his property.

60. After such long and careful observation of Earth, such a race would know a great deal about us and our way of life and our scientific achievements. Because of this, I am sure they would be careful not to be caught off guard should we visit them eventually.

61. It is thoughts of this nature that convince me that the rejection of our current hypothesis on grounds of the lack of answers to questions such as why don't they land, why don't they contact us etc., is a major error in our thinking. **Our** way of doing things must not be taken as a standard for others, particularly those who may be far more advanced in all ways. It is therefore unreasonable, in my view, to reject the interplanetary hypothesis on philosophical grounds.

A POLICY DECISION IS NEEDED

62. It is well for us to bear in mind that Science, by its very nature, is forever prevented from solving some problems. Although science assists us in controlling nature, it is unable to guide us in determining in what direction we should exercise such control. With respect to the external world, science is our guide to a means to an end, but it has no part in determining the ends to which means should be directed.

63. It is in this regard that I state that the decision as to whether a thorough, complete and objective study of the UFO enigma is to be carried out is a governmental decision and should be based upon the possible benefits or otherwise, to humanity, which might accrue from the solving of the mystery. If, for instance, UFOs are interplanetary space ships, thus proving that other worlds are inhabited by beings supe-

rior, in at least some ways, to us on Earth, with a science and technology far in advance of ours, there are benefits to the human race here if we can also acquire this knowledge. Clearly, a decision to embark upon a program to solve this mystery is not solely a scientific decision, and therefore, conversely, a decision **not** to embark upon such a program should not be based upon scientific advice alone. There are moral, ethical, economic, and philosophical considerations also, which are at least equally as important as the scientific ones, as these represent end results to be gained, in addition to scientific and technological advancement. Questions are also raised regarding the future, and past, of the human race on Earth. Dr. Carl Sagan told a committee of the U.S. House of Representatives that "a bonafide example of extraterrestrial life even in a very simple form would revolutionize biology . . . it would have both practical and fundamental scientific benefits."[31]

64. Data collected on erratically-moving phenomena (including the rapid determination of any landings or impacts) would add significantly to the coverage and analyses of meteorites, as well as contributing to an understanding of atmospheric physics, one of the great mysteries of which is ball lightning.

65. Also, although there is no current basis for concluding that hostility and grave hazard lie behind the UFO mystery, we cannot be entirely sure of that. A risk we are taking is the possibility that UFOs may be mistaken for hostile devices of another nation on Earth which might accidentally trigger a nuclear war.

66. For all of these reasons greatly expanded scientific and public attention to the UFO problem is urgently needed. I suggest that lack of governmental action in the past has been due, primarily, to negative scientific favour for such a program. To date, it seems that the Science Council of Canada has ignored the UFO problem, which in effect means the Council is ignoring the benefits which could accrue from solving the mystery.

67. Humanitarian considerations should be the real objective of all scientific advance, otherwise there is no point to scientific inquiry. Knowledge for its own sake is useless—it must be put to use for mankind's benefit. We surely want to

134

advance the human race, so all research should be directed with this aim in mind. If societies on other planets are far advanced over us, we can learn from them, thus saving ourselves a great deal of effort and money.

68. There was a program in the U.S.A. to seek out life on other planets and I emphasize **on** other planets. This method was by means of radio. But if such alien life is, perhaps, transporting itself to our own atmosphere, it would appear more logical to seek it out right here, in our own supposedly-familiar environment than tens of millions of miles away. The chance of finding alien life here (if it is visiting us) seems to be infinitely greater.

69. If UFOs are some unknown natural atmospheric phenomena then we are not as familiar with our own environment as we think, so we should be trying harder to learn more about it. This could explain the inability of our meteorological experts to give us more accurate weather forecasts. It is a fact that several aircraft have crashed while chasing UFOs and their crews have been killed. Many near-collisions in the air are on record. As stated before, UFOs have been seen over the location of huge power blackouts. After all these years is it not time that science had an answer for us? What tragedies can we expect in future while science in general continues to ignore this situation?.

70. As an argument against the existence of visiting interplanetary vehicles I have been told by scientists that if life exists on other planets, any communication with such civilizations is more likely to begin by radio techniques than by space vehicles. In my opinion, there are at least two things wrong with this view. First, it assumes that because this may be more likely, the possibility of space vehicle communication may be ignored. Secondly, it overlooks the possibility that attempts to communicate with us by radio may have been started thousands of years ago, even before space vehicles may have begun visiting us. Because we have not been aware of radio messages to us does not by any means prove that such attempts have not been made. Certainly, until just a few years ago, we weren't even listening!

71. It is now known that Russian scientists are engaged in a UFO inquiry, as referred to earlier. This is of particular

significance in that western nations could be placed in a most embarrassing position if Russia should be the first to discover that UFOs are indeed intelligently-controlled interplanetary space vehicles, and announces this, along with its evidence, to the entire world. Russia could, indeed, become the first nation to make contact with such a race. Russia might acquire this knowledge and not share it with the remainder of the world, but use it to further her own ends alone. This possibility in itself is sufficient justification for all nations to work together to solve the mystery and share the benefits equally. As Dr. James McDonald stated:

"It would be amusing if it should turn out that Russian scientists are the ones who finally convince the world that twenty years of assurances by the United States Air Force were completely unjustified."[32]

72. I have attempted to show to you that the UFO phenomenon is of far wider scope than is generally recognized. It embraces much more than just a few fields of science and overflows into areas not yet within the bounds of science. The scientists themselves, generally speaking, are limited by their own fields of specialization. Whole aspects of the problem are overlooked, if humanitarian considerations are omitted. And these are omitted in purely scientific studies. Unless all the many aspects of the problem are considered as a part of the total problem, a distorted view of the overall picture is bound to be the result. This has proved to be so.

73. This is the age of the specialist, the expert, the professional, and it has become increasingly the age of the jealously-guarded vested interests in all spheres of activity. The average layman has been made to feel inferior, by degrees, credentials and authorities in all professional areas and the experts have encouraged this awe of authority as it boosts their status in the public eye.

74. The average citizen lacks the courage to openly disagree with the "experts" because of this air of authority which they carry. The UFO phenomenon has been left in the care of the supposed "experts" for twenty years and they have not reached a solution to it. It is time for a broader view to be taken of this great mystery, unrestricted by the narrow fields of specialization of particular individuals.

75. It was Dr. Rene Dubos, of the Rockefeller Institute for Medical Research who stated:

"A society that blindly accepts the decisions of experts is a sick society. The time has come when we must produce, alongside specialists another class of scholars and citizens who have broad familiarity with the facts, methods and objectives of science, and thus are capable of making judgments about scientific policies."[33]

76. The public is growing impatient and does not want another twenty years of UFO confusion. They want to know if there really is something to this whole business—and they are dissatisfied with answers handed out to them. The public in general may lack detailed knowledge of scientific matters but they have an uncanny way of distinguishing between an honest scientific approach and the method of ridicule. If ours is to be a "just society" then it is time for the people to be given all the facts. It is time for a top level recognition of the UFO phenomenon as a matter of extreme importance to the human race on this planet. This recognition must be followed up by a determination to discover for certain what UFOs really are.

77. In my opinion the hypothesis I have been discussing remains the only hypothesis which remains valid to explain **all** UFOs at this time. This hypothesis must be retained until proved wrong, or one is proposed which is better able to explain **all** the observed facts.

78. To test this hypothesis, we need a proper investigation, not limited as past and present inquiries have been. All the numerous areas of the matter which I identified in my book must be a part of such investigation. Sightings need to be properly and thoroughly reported and co-ordinated. A move is underway in the U.S.A. to get thousands of ham radio operators to transmit sighting reports immediately so that others may watch for these objects as they are reported travelling in certain directions so that plots of their movements may be made, to establish patterns of activity.[34] Certain patterns have already been established in some parts of the world, and organizing in this manner could be very helpful in collecting the necessary data for computer pro-

137

cessing. Patterns are needed in the scientific investigation of UFOs. Will Oursler stated:
"A case by case acceptance or refutation of individual sightings is of little value. We need to explore the possible underlying meanings of these sightings to search for some pattern that might provide a reasonable hypothesis for as yet unexplored avenues of further examination."[35]

79. Some patterns already observed by private investigators, include observations along great circle routes, electromagnetic (EM) interference, physiological effects, the locality of terrestrial significance and colour changes, among others. There now appears to be evidence for a developing pattern which links UFOs to fault lines in the earth's crust. As seismologists know, it is here that many major earthquakes occur. If such a pattern is confirmed, this could be of considerable significance.

80. There are many things that need doing in the conduct of such an investigation. Detection of patterns is only one example.

81. As stated earlier, one substantial sighting, properly verified, proves that UFOs exist. 10,000 sightings don't prove it any further. But the 10,000 sightings might establish what they are, and this is the question that now requires a definite answer. The other question that must be answered in conjunction with that one is, what are they doing here? As these objects are busying themselves all over the world, they must be doing **something**. We need to know what that something is; what the purpose is behind their activities; what they are really doing that requires frequent landings in remote areas; what requires the widespread and primarily nocturnal activity.

82. As UFOs are a world-wide phenomenon, and the patterns are observed on a global basis, the mystery must be studied on a global basis in order to establish full and complete patterns. This, of course, requires international co-operation, with a central co-ordination or "filter" centre. I suggest that the UN, as a detached, international organization is the ideal organization to do this. But before the UN would undertake such a task, it is to be expected, I would think, that individual nations show strong concern over the prob-

lem and demonstrate a desire to solve it by taking some positive action in that direction.

83. I therefore suggest that we in Canada awaken from our slumber and realize the importance of the matter and attempt to solve this mystery on a **total** basis, with a fully-objective study, not limited to narrow fields as in the past, and not restricted to an individual-sighting basis. The UFO presents a direct challenge to the physical and philosophical concepts developed by man over many years. The final analysis of our own existence could be dependent upon the sincerity with which we conduct this research. Scientists should accept as a challenge the opportunity to be a part of a formal inquiry into UFOs. Such an inquiry should include serious laymen researchers as well as scientists, as it is important that the two groups work together, rather than against each other. There are private researchers and organized groups in possession, collectively, of a vast amount of scientific and technical data, and detailed, fully-investigated sighting reports, far in excess of that possessed by governments, in my opinion. As so much valuable data is already in the hands of such non-official researchers, it would be a major error to ignore it. I have seen no evidence that either NRC or the University of Toronto have collected this data from other groups in order to conduct an adequate study. And let it not be forgotten that such data has been collected all over the world and the total accumulation is monumental.

84. The public has been confused by reported sightings made by reliable and trusted citizens on the one hand, and official refutations on the other. Thousands of people feel that officialdom is not being honest with them and they want the answer as to what UFOs really are—the right answer. This situation must be brought to an end so that all the known facts can be made available to the public. The UFO mystery is a matter of national and international importance and must be given the attention it deserves.

85. In order to accomplish this, I specifically recommend that Canada's science policy include serious and urgent consideration of the UFO enigma. Science cannot escape this phenomenon—it is merely shying away from it in an effort

to avoid it. This policy should include the determination to solve the mystery in concert with other nations, and set the example to other nations by establishing the first fully-objective, and open investigations, not shrouded in a cloak of secrecy, which will leave no stones unturned in getting to the heart of the matter. Funds must be provided in order that the right answer can be found. Our example to other nations should then provide the necessary encouragement for them to join us in this exciting quest so that eventually the UN can be the global co-ordinator for the study.

86. Science works with models. Models are constructed as a means of explaining phenomena. What is needed, is not a model UFO, but a new model of the universe. Existing accepted models of the universe are designed to explain the known facts of physics. We are aware that there is a great deal that we do not know. The unknown may or may not be explainable by existing models.

87. I suggest we need a model which will permit interstellar flight in brief time periods. It might have to include an entirely new concept of time, and probably also, new dimensions. It would require the postulation of new theoretical concepts and, perhaps, the discarding of some existing laws on the grounds that they are too restrictive, and are valid only within known conditions.

88. To show that my suggestion may not be as "far out" as it may at first appear, I will quote Dr. T. Gold of Cornell University:

"Introspective understanding of the flow of time is basic to all our physics, and yet it is not clear how this idea of time is derived, or what status it ought to have in the description of the physical world."

"It may be that no very profound improvement in our understanding of time will ever take place, but it could also be that some new physical theory will be devised one day that depends on, or defines, a different concept of time."[36] Perhaps when we gain a true understanding of the real nature of time, we will find that lengthy periods are not involved in interstellar travel after all.

89. Let the construction of a new model of the universe be a challenge to science in Canada. This can be done as an

140

intellectual exercise without the expenditure of large sums of money. As the Government is engaged in a cutback in spending, we might achieve great things at very little cost. We could achieve far more than with the Intense Neutron Generator which was to have cost us in the neighbourhood of $150,000,000 initially. Let us put our best scientific brains to work on theoretical cosmology without delay. The prestige to be enjoyed by Canada in the eyes of the world if we should be the ones to discover new physical laws, and to build a new model of the universe, would be tremendous, and we will then have grown to giant scientific stature.

QUESTIONS AND ANSWERS ABOUT THE
"CONDON REPORT"

1. The Scientific Study of Unidentified Flying Objects was conducted by the University of Colorado, under contract to the United States Air Force, under the direction of Dr. Edward U. Condon. The Final Report, commonly referred to as the "Condon Report" was published by Bantam Books, New York, in January, 1969, under the title "Scientific Study of Unidentified Flying Objects" and contains the complete text of the original edition. Not one word has been omitted, according to the publisher.

2. As a result of the general impression conveyed by press reports that the investigation proved that there is nothing significant to UFO sightings, listed below are a few of the questions which must be asked concerning the "Condon Report", with the answers provided by the Report.

Notes:
1. Every effort has been made not to take quotations out of the general context of the Report.
2. Page references refer to the Bantam Edition of the Report.

Question 1. Does the Report claim to give the "final answer" to what all UFOs are?
    A. No.

Question 2. Does the Report add anything to scientific knowledge?
    A. No.

Question 3. Did the Committee encourage or solicit submission of sighting reports by the public?
    A. No. (p. 11).

Question 4. Approximately what percentage of all sightings were reported to the Committee?
    A. Approximately 10% at most. (p. 11).

Question 5. Did the Committee investigate all reports that were received?

A. No. "Our available resources for field study enabled us to deal only with a small fraction of the reports coming in", (p. 11). (i.e. a small fraction of the 10% reported).

Question 6. Was the Committee able to to explain satisfactorily all or nearly all cases which were investigated?

A. "A common situation was one in which the lack of evidence made the investigation totally inconclusive" (p. 61).

Question 7. Were there any cases investigated which could be explained **only** in terms of "strange vehicles"?

A. "The label 'unidentified' does not necessarily imply that an unusual or strange object was present. On the other hand, some cases involve testimony, which, if taken at face value describes experiences which can be explained only in terms of the presence of strange vehicles . . . These cases are puzzling and conclusions regarding them depend entirely upon the weight one gives to the personal testimony as presented." (p. 62).

Question 8. Did the investigation determine that most UFO witnesses are emotionally disturbed or irresponsble people?

A. "In our experience, the persons making reports seem in nearly all cases to be normal, responsible individuals. In most cases they are quite calm, at least by the time they make a report. They are simply puzzled about what they saw and hope that they can be helped to a better understanding of it. Only a very few are obviously quite emotionally disturbed, their minds being filled with pseudo-scientific, pseudo-religious or other fantasies. Cases of this kind range from slight disturbance to those who are manifestly in need of psychiatric care. The latter form an extremely small minority of all the persons encountered in this study. While the existence of a few mentally unbalanced persons among UFO observers is part of the total situation, it is completely incorrect and unfair to imply that all who report UFOs are "crazy kooks", just as it is equally incorrect to ignore the fact that

143

there are mentally disturbed persons among them". (p. 10).

Question 9. Is it expected that the conclusions of the "Condon Report" will meet with general agreement among scientists?

A. "If they (other scientists) disagree (with the conclusions) it will be because our report has helped them reach a clear picture of wherein existing studies are faulty or incomplete and thereby will have stimulated ideas for more accurate studies. If they do get such ideas and can formulate them clearly, we have no doubt that support will be forthcoming to carry on with such clearly-defined, specific studies. We think that such ideas for work should be supported." (p. 2). (Insertions in parentheses made by author of this brief).

Question 10. Did the Committee find that Project Blue Book had done an adequate job of investigating UFOs?

A. "Material on a number of older cases was obtained from the Aerial Phenomena Office (Project Bue Book) at Wright-Patterson Air Force Base, Ohio. In many cases, these files were not sufficiently organized or complete to permit an intelligent evaluation of the report." (p. 76).

STATEMENT PREPARED FOR MINISTER OF TRANSPORT
RE PROJECT MAGNET

In view of the somewhat sensational articles appearing in the press as to some of the researches being carried out by the Department of Transport, I wish to outline to Members of the House the scope of such undertakings.

The Department of Transport receives from time to time a variety of reasonably authenticated reports of strange objects, lights or queer effects in the sky. All reports of such phenomenae are carefully checked, analysed, and catalogued for their possible scientific value. Many of the sightings, as may be expected, turn out to be perfectly normal objects or phenomenae, but there are a few which apparently represent something new in the field of science, in that there is no ready-made explanation for them. These are the ones of particular interest and on which we would like to have further and more scientific information. Several theories have been advanced in an effort to explain these more difficult sightings, and we can choose between these theories only through experiment and observation. We do not know what the unexplained sightings represent, but in this day and age when every available avenue of research is being explored, it would be remiss to ignore this field.

The Telecommunications Division of the Department of Transport have been studying for some time the characteristics and behaviour of the atmosphere in connection with radio wave propagation studies, which are vitally necessary in the face of a rapidly expanding radio art. The Division had left over from a previous program of radio skywave recording, a number of instruments which could be adapted for a study of certain aspects of the unidentified objects and kindred phenomenae. The modifications were made and the instruments set up in a hut near the Ionospheric Measurement Station at Shirley Bay.

This installation is in no sense unusual since most of the instruments are quite conventional. There is a gamma ray counter which will detect the presence of radioactive or cosmic radiation; a magnetometer which will register variations or disturbances in the earth's magnetic field; a radio receiver to detect the presence of radio noise; and a recording gravimeter which will detect any variations in the earth's gravitational pull. These four instruments produce traces on a multiple pen graphical recorder, the charts from which will be scrutinized from time to time for any disturbances which may appear.

This entire program of collecting data on sightings of unidentified flying objects, their analysis, and the associated investigational work is being carried on by a small group in the Telecommunications Division of the Department of Transport, with official approval and authority to make use of existing facilities. They are not assigned exclusively to this work, and in fact much of the work has been done on their own time. It is much too early to expect data from the Shirley Bay station, or even to indicate what the measurements, if any, will show. From the past record of sightings it is probable that the station may not be called upon to function for many months, and even so, it may not be set up to measure the correct thing.

June 25, 1952

INTERIM REPORT PROJECT MAGNET

Project Magnet was established November 21, 1950 by authority of Commander C. P. Edwards, then Deputy Minister of Transport for Air Services. Prior to this date some research in magnetic phenomena had been carried out in the Department of Transport in connection with radio wave propagation studies, and an indication had been obtained that the subject comprised a promising field for investigation.

The large number of sightings of unidentified objects generally called "Flying Saucers", and the intimation that they operate on some kind of magnetic principles, raised the question as to whether or not our investigations in the field of magnetics could be extended to a study of the saucers in the hope that we might uncover the technology which made them possible. Permission was sought and obtained to carry out further researches within the framework of the existing Standards Laboratory establishment, and a small working group set up on a part time basis to study the saucer problem and gain a perspective on the matter.

One of the terms of reference of the project was to study the various saucer sighting reports to determine if there was any consistent behaviour from which their operating principles might be deduced. Since their operation was suspected to be in some way magnetic, studies were directed in the theoretical field, with particular reference to those aspects which may have received only casual investigation while our present technology was developing.

The limited amount of information available regarding the flying saucers has proven a serious handicap in evaluating the characteristics and salient features of this possible other technology. Furthermore, the complete absence of specimens has made a direct approach impossible. The source of data for these studies was almost entirely information published in the Press. Such other information as was obtained was useful primarily in establishing the reality of the saucers.

From the available data, the following composite description of a typical saucer was built up.

General shape:	Thin round disc with hemispherical bulge on one side.
Dimensions:	Diameter 100 to 200 feet; thickness in center about 10 feet: thickness of rim, probably 2 feet.
Material:	Glassy, metallic, with extremely high co-efficient of reflection for visible light (or on occasion, self luminous).
Operating position:	Any, and without regard to the relation between the plane of the disc and the direction of motion.
Speed:	Capable of extremely high speeds, well into the supersonic range, probably as high as 18,000 miles per hour.
Power:	Unknown, but certainly not chemical jets, or atomic with fission products ejected.
Magnetic:	Magnetic disturbances sufficient to influence compass needle at about 10 miles distance.
Noise:	Completely absent, except for possible slight swish.
Electrical:	Sometimes appear to be surrounded by corona.

The foregoing description seems to fit the majority of actual saucer sightings, although it is quite possible that several types of saucers may exist. The variety in the descriptions is probably due to the angle of observation, and the relative position of the saucer. One point which seems to be significant is that the saucers did not always move in the same direction relative to the plane of the disc.

As a starting point and as a working hypothesis it was assumed that the driving and sustaining force was the simple interaction between an electric current and the earth's magnetic field. But any electric currents with which we are familiar must complete some sort of a circuit, and the force on the complete circuit in a magnetic field is a turning moment, not a unidirectional force. The unidirectional force on the circuit could only appear if the magnetic field were either increasing or decreasing towards

148

some point not in the plane of the circuit. This implies the existence of a magnetic "source" or "sink", which is basically contrary to our concepts of magnetism. However, if the existence of such a phenomenon could be conceded, the design of the saucers is entirely consistent, and their behaviour even more so.

With this concept in mind a study was undertaken of the fundamental behaviour of magnetic fields to see if some discrepancy could be found which would permit the existence of a magnetic sink within the framework of classical electricity and magnetism.

We as human beings, have no sense by which we can detect or observe a magnetic field. We know of the existence of such fields only through the effects which they produce and which we can observe, either directly or indirectly. We therefore know little or nothing about the actual structure of such fields. The first point questioned was the validity of assuming that when we have measured the resultant effect of a number of fields, we have in fact measured the effect of a resultant field. And further, that a number of fields producing a resultant effect which we can measure may not in actual fact combine to form a resultant field, but continue their independent existence.

The independent existence of magnetic fields was confirmed by the following experiment. Two coils, A and B were made up from small diameter concentric line, and arranged so that equal currents could be sent through them and through large series inductances. Coil B was shunted by a ballistic galvanometer in series with a condenser. A resultant magnetic field was measured by an ordinary flux meter, when either coil was carrying current, but when the two coils were carrying equal currents the flux meter indicated zero field. The energy, $\frac{1}{2}LI^2$, in inductance B was measured with and without current flowing in A, and found to be identical. From this it was concluded that, (a) magnetic fields existed independently, or (b) the energy does not reside in the magnetic field, or both.

It was therefore concluded that the concept of the vectorial addition of incremental magnetic fields to form a resultant, does not truly represent the actual structure of such fields, but is a concept of convenience which fortunately makes little or no difference in most practical cases.

149

The question of the mechanism by which magnetic fields become established in magnetic materials was studied by winding two small coils on opposite sides of a powdered iron toroid, and exciting one of them with high frequency current. The phase angle was carefully measured between the exciting current and the emf induced in the other coil and the corresponding time lag determined. This time lag corresponded with the time required for the magnetic field to flash across the window of the toroid, rather than to go the long way round through the magnetic material. Thus it was concluded that magnetic fields propagate by lateral motion, and Maxwell's equations could be expected to hold for these cases.

Maxwell's equations were investigated to see if they could be extended in some manner which would make permissible a magnetic sink, and still conform with the foregoing concepts. This investigation was not entirely successful, but the various possibilities are far from being exhausted and the work is still proceeding.

There are a number of implications to the blanket application of the foregoing principles, which must be sorted out. For instance, the Maxwellian propagation of magnetic fields requires a rather special mechanism for the magnetization of a magnetic material, involving three waves, and two kinds of permeability. Consider a conductor placed near a body of magnetic material, and that one of the electrons in the conductor be started in motion causing a minute current to flow. The acceleration of the electron would send outward a Hertzian wave which would ride out along the radial electric field to an indefinite distance. The velocity of propagation of this wave would be $\frac{c}{\sqrt{u_1 k_1}}$ where c is the velocity of light in vacuo, u_1 the instantaneous permeability of the region through which the wave passes, and k_1 the instantaneous dielectric constant of the same region. However, as the wave passes through the magnetic material, the magnetic vector will encounter and exert forces upon many individual fields already existing within the material, and the electric vector will also encounter and exert forces upon many individual electric charges. However, these small fields and charges will require a finite time to move under the influence of the exciting field. When they do move, however, each will send outward its own Hertzian wave which in turn will operate on all the other fields,

150

and so on. The net result of all this will be the generation of two more waves within the magnetic material which will propagate through it in opposite directions, one in the same direction as the exciting wave and the other in the reverse direction. There will be a substantial time lag between the passing of the exciting wave and the passing of the secondary waves, which could be interpreted as resulting from a different velocity of propagation within the material, $\dfrac{c}{\sqrt{u_2 k_2}}$. This interpretation would be valid only so long as it is remembered that u_2 and k_2 are functions of time. But if it is considered that the secondary wave is actually made up of many separate individual waves, then u_2 and k_2 would become constants for each wave.

An answer which is required but not yet found deals with the energy exchange between a charged particle and the surrounding field, when the particle is undergoing acceleration, either positive or negative. It appears that the space surrounding matter is filled with myriads of electric and magnetic fields, the former describing the position of the material particle and the latter describing its state of motion. The relative behaviour of these fields would therefore be representative of the relative potential and kinetic energy respectively. Consequently, when a particle changes its relative position or motion, such change must be reflected in its fields. The question which arises at this point is the actual whereabouts of the energy involved; is it in the particle itself, its fields or some intermediate state? Also, since the position and motion of a particle are relative, are the energies also relative, and if so, how is this relativity reflected in its fields? Again, since we observe that Hertzian waves do contain energy, but have peculiar characteristics in other respects, and that magnetic fields get into place through this mechanism, we have another large question, are the electric fields and magnetic fields associated with the position and motion of a particle IDENTICAL with the electric and magnetic fields making up a Hertzian wave?

Various lines of reasoning may be followed with respect to the foregoing, each leading to interesting conclusions. It is necessary of course to devise experiments to obtain as direct answers as possible to the queries posed above and others that follow as a logical consequence, before any definite conclusions can be reached. However, it does appear that in the evolution of our technology we did not give sufficient attention to the actual structure of fields, and therefore missed a good many interesting and probably very useful facts. We can backtrack, however, in the light of our knowledge and pick up these facts. If, as appears evident, the Flying Saucers are emissaries from some other civilization, and actually do operate on magnetic principles, we have before us the Fact that we have missed something in magnetic theory but have a good indication of the direction in which to look for the missing quantities. It is therefore strongly recommended that the work of Project Magnet be continued and expanded to include experts in each of the various fields involved in these studies.

(W. B. Smith)
Senior Radio Engineer
Broadcast and Measurements Section.

ANNEX 4

PROJECT MAGNET REPORT

During the past five years there has been accumulating in the files of the United States Air Force, Royal Canadian Air Force, Department of Transport, and various other agencies, an impressive number of reports on sightings of unidentified flying objects popularly known as "Flying Saucers". These files contain reports by creditable people on things which they have seen in the sky, tracked by radar, or photographed. They are reports made in good faith by normal, honest people, and there is little if any reason to doubt their veracity. Many sightings undoubtedly are due to unusual views of common objects or phenomenae, and are quite normal, but there are many sightings which cannot be explained so easily.

Project Magnet was authorized in December, 1950, by Commander C. P. Edwards, then Deputy Minister of Transport for Air Services, for the purpose of making as detailed a study of the saucer phenomenae as could be made within the framework of existing establishments. The Broadcast and Measurements Section of the Telecommunications Division were given the directive to go ahead with this work with whatever assistance could be obtained informally from outside sources such as Defence Research Board and National Research Council.

It is perfectly natural in the human thinking mechanism to try and fit observations into an established pattern. It is only when observations stubbornly refuse to be so fitted that we become disturbed. When this happens we may, and usually do, take one of three courses. First, we may deny completely the validity of the observations; or second, we may pass the whole subject off as something of no consequence; or third, we may accept the discrepancies as real and go to work on them. In the matter of Saucer Sightings all three of these reactions have been strikingly apparent. The first two approaches are obviously negative and from which a definite conclusion can never be reached. It is the third approach, acceptance of the data and subsequent research that is dealt with in this report.

The basic data with which we have to work consist largely of sightings reported as they are observed throughout Canada in a

153

purely random manner. Many of the reports are from the extensive field organization of the Department of Transport whose job it is to watch the sky and whose observers are trained in precisely this sort of observation. Also, there are in operation a number of instrumental arrangements such as the ionospheric observatories from which useful data have been obtained. However, we must not expect too much from these field stations because of the very sporadic nature of the sightings. As the analysis progresses and we know more about what to look for we may be able to obtain and make much better use of field data. Up to the present we have been prevented from using conventional laboratory methods owing to the complete lack of any sort of specimens with which to experiment, and our prospects of obtaining any in the immediate future are not very good. Consequently, a large part of the analysis in these early stages will have to be based on deductive reasoning, at least until we are able to work out a procedure more in line with conventional experimental methods.

The starting point of the investigation is essentially the interview with an observer. A questionnaire form and an instructional guide for the interrogator were worked out by the Project Second Storey Committee, which is a Committee sponsored by the Defence Research Board to collect, catalogue and correlate data on sightings of unidentified flying objects. This questionnaire and guide are included as Appendix I, and are intended to get the maximum useful information from the observer and present it in a manner in which it can be used to advantage. This form has been used so far as possible in connection with the sightings investigated by the Department of Transport.

A weighting factor is assigned to each sighting according to a system intended to minimize the personal equation. This weighting system is described in Appendix II. The weighting factor may be considered as the probability that the report contains the truth, the whole truth and nothing but the truth, so far as the observer and interrogator are aware. It has nothing to do with the nature of the object claimed to be seen. It is in a sense analogous to the order of precision with which a measurement may be made, and for the purpose of this analysis this is precisely the manner in which it is used.

Sightings may be grouped according to certain salient features, and the combined weight of all pertinent observations with respect to these features may be determined by applying Peter's formula, which is a standard mathematical technique for determining probable error.

$$r_o = \frac{.8453}{n \sqrt{n-1}} \; (v_1 + v_2 + v_3 + \ldots v_n) .$$

where r_o is the probable error of the mean, n is the number of observations and v is the probable error of each observation, that is, unity minus the weighting factor. This method has the advantage of being simple and easy to use and enables a number of mediocre observations to be combined effectively into the equivalent of one good one.

The next step is to sort out the observations according to some pattern. The particular pattern is not so important as the fact that it should take account of all contingencies however improbable they may appear at first sight. In other words, there must be a compartment somewhere in the scheme of things into which each sighting may be placed, comfortably, and with nothing left over. Furthermore, it must be possible to arrive at each appropriate compartment by a sequence of logical reasoning taking account of all the facts presented. If this can be done, then the probability for the real existance of the contents of any compartment will be the single or combined weighting factor pertinent to that single or group of sightings. The charts shown in Appendix III were evolved as a means for sorting out the various sightings and provide the pattern which was used in the analysis of those sightings reported to and analysed by the Department of Transport.

Most sightings fit readily into one of the classifications shown, which are of two general types; those about which we know something and those about which we know very little. When the sightings can be classified as something we know about, we need not concern ourselves too much with them, but when they fit into classifications which we don't understand we are back to our original position of whether to deny the evidence, dismiss it as of no consequence, or to accept it and go to work on it. The process of sorting out observations according to these charts and fitting them into compartments can hardly be considered an end in itself. Rather, it is a convenience to clarify thinking and direct activity along profitable channels. It shows at once which àspects are of significance and which may be bypassed. Merely placing a sighting under a certain heading does not explain it; it only indicates where we may start looking for an explanation.

Appendix IV contains summaries of the 1952 sightings as investigated by the Department of Transport. Considerably more data exists in the files of other agencies, and more is being collected as the investigations proceed. While it is not intended to make any reference to an analysis of the records of other agencies, it may be said that the Department of Transport sightings are quite representative of the sightings reported throughout the world. The following is a table of the breakdown of the 25 proper sightings reported during 1952.

NATURE OF SIGHTING	NUMBER	WEIGHT
Probably meteor	4	91%
Probably aircraft	1	69%
Probably balloons	1	74%
Probably marker light	1	64%
Bright speck at night, not star or planet	3	75%
Bright speck daylight, not star or planet	1	68%
Luminous ring	1	68%
Shiny cone	1	53%
Circular or elliptical body, shiny day	5	88%
Circular or elliptical body luminous night	5	90%
Unidentified lights of various kinds	2	77%
TOTAL NUMBER OF PROPER SIGHTINGS	25	96%

With reference to the above table, of the four cases identified as probably meteors, their weight works out at 91%, which is the probability that the observers actually did see meteors which appeared as they described them. Considering the circular or elliptical bodies together, their weight works out at 91% for the ten sightings, from which we may conclude that SOMETHING answering this description was actually observed. Similarly we may consider each of the other groups of sightings, taking account of the probability that the observations are reliable.

It is not intended to describe here in detail the intricate and tedious processes by which the sightings are evaluated, beyond the fact that the pattern set forth in the charts in Appendix III is followed. The cardinal rule is that a sighting must fit completely under one or more of the chart headings, with nothing left over and without postulating any additions, deletions, or changes in the facts as reported. Should there be no suitable heading, then obviously the charts must be expanded to provide one, in fact this was the evolution of these charts. Where a sighting may be fitted under more than one heading an arbitrary division of the probability of finding it under each applicable heading is assigned. The sum of such probability figures must of course be unity, and the probability for the real existence under any particular heading is the product of this probability figure and the reliability or weighting factor for the sighting concerned.

It is apparent that the judgement of the people doing the evaluating is bound to enter the picture and may produce substantial numerical differences with reference to sightings listed under certain headings. However, since many headings are automatically eliminated by the nature of the facts available, the discrepancies are confined to the probability figures for the distribution under the remaining headings which are considered eligible, and we end up with definite classifications for the sightings with SOME probability figure for the reality of each group. This has the effect of forcing those who are doing the evaluating to face the reported facts squarely, pay meticulous attention to them, and place each sighting honestly under the only headings where it will fit.

In working through the analysis of the proper sightings listed, we find that the majority of them appear to be of some material body. Of these, seven are classed as probably normal objects, and eleven are classed as strange objects. Of the remainder, four have a substantial probability of being material, strange, objects, with three having a substantial probability of being immaterial, electrical, phenomenae. Of the eleven strange objects the probability definitely favours the alien vehicle class, with the secret missile included with a much lower probability.

The next step is to follow this line of reasoning as far as possible so as to deduce what we can from the observed data. Vehicles or missiles can be of only two general kinds, terrestrial and extra-terrestrial, and in either case the analysis enquires into the source and technology. If the vehicles originate outside the iron curtain we may assume that the matter is in good hands, but if they originate inside the iron curtain it could be a matter of grave concern to us.

In the matter of technology, the points of interest are: — the energy source; means of support, propulsion and manipulation; structure; and biology. So far as energy is concerned we know about mechanical energy and chemical energy, and a little about energy of fission, and we can appreciate the possibility of direct conversion of mass to energy. Beyond this we have no knowledge, and unless we are prepared to postulate a completely unknown source of energy of which we do not know even the rudiments, we must conclude that the vehicles use one of the four listed energy sources. Unless something we do not understand can be done with gravitation, mechanical energy has little use beyond driving model aircraft. We use chemical energy to quite an extent, but we realize its limitations, so if the energy demands of the vehicles exceed what we consider to be the reasonable capabilities of chemical fuels, we are forced to the conclusion that such vehicles must get their energy from either fission or mass conversion.

With reference to the means for support, propulsion and manipulation, unless we are prepared to postulate something else quite beyond our knowledge, there are only the two groups of possibilities, namely the known means and the speculative means. Of the known means there is only physical support through the use of buoyancy or airfoils, the reaction of rockets and jets, and centrifugal force, which is what holds the moon in position. Of the speculative means we know only of the possibility of gravity waves, field interaction and radiation pressure. If the observed behaviour of the vehicles is such as to be beyond the limitations which we know apply to the known means of support, then we are forced to the conclusion that one of the speculative means must have been developed to do the job.

From a study of the sighting reports (Appendix IV), it can be deduced that the vehicles have the following significant characteristics. They are a hundred feet or more in diameter; they can travel at speeds of several thousand miles per hour; they can reach altitudes well above those which would support conventional aircraft or balloons; and ample power and force seem to be available for all required manoeuvres. Taking these factors into account, it is difficult to reconcile this performance with the capabilities of our technology, and unless the technology of some terrestrial nation is much more advanced than is generally known, we are forced to the conclusion that the vehicles are probably extra-terrestrial, in spite of our prejudices to the contrary.

It has been suggested that the sightings might be due to some sort of optical phenomenon which gives the appearance of the objects reported, and this aspect was thoroughly investigated. Charts are shown in Appendix III showing the various optical considerations. Enticing as this theory is, there are some serious objections to its actual application, in the form of some rather definite and quite immutable optical laws. These are the geometrical laws dealing with optics generally and which we have never yet found cause to doubt, plus the wide discrepancies in the order of magnetude (sic) of the light values which must be involved in any sightings so far studied. Furthermore, introducing an optical system might explain an image in terms of an object, but the object still requires explaining. A particular effort was made to find an optical explanation for the sightings listed in this report, but in no case could one be worked out. It was not possible to find so much as a partial optical explanation for even one sighting. Consequently, it was felt that optical theories generally should not be taken too seriously until such time as at least one sighting can be satisfactorily explained in such a manner.

It appears then, that we are faced with a substantial probability of the real existence of extra-terrestrial vehicles, regardless of whether or not they fit into our scheme of things. Such vehicles of necessity must use a technology considerably in advance of what we have. It is therefore submitted that the next step in this investigation should be a substantial effort towards the acquisition of as much as possible of this technology, which would without doubt be of great value to us.

W. B. Smith,
Engineer-in-Charge,
Project Magnet.

APPENDIX I

PROJECT SECOND STOREY

Part I—Information for guidance in reporting on unknown flying objects.

In collecting data on unknown flying objects, accuracy of observation and record is of prime importance. The observer should report carefully and precisely what he sees and hears with a minimum of private personal interpretation. Accurate numerical data to the best of the observer's ability are most desirable. Confirmation of the observation by others is also desirable, particularly if other observers are located some distance away so that they may have a slightly different view of the object.

The sighting report is for the purpose of obtaining specific information regarding a particular sighting. Most of the questions are straightforward and call for an obvious answer. Some questions, however, may require a certain amount of explanation so that the required information may be forthcoming. It should be noted that the information obtained will not be made public.

The following headings refer to numbered questions on the Project Second Storey Sighting Report Form.

A. (3) Occupation and Previous Relevant Experience
Note: State if the observer has had any previous experience, for example, as an observer in the Air Force or as an amateur astronomer, or as an employee at a Government Weather Station.

B. (7) Date and Local Time
The exact date and time, whether Local, Standard, or Daylight Saving Time of a sighting should be specified. Where possible the accuracy of the time piece should be determined.

B. (8) Position of observer as accurately as possible.
The exact position of the observer during the sighting should be noted as accurately as possible, with particular reference to nearby objects such as buildings, trees, etc. Where possible the exact latitude and longitude of the point of observation should be

given. If this is not known the point should be indicated on a convenient map.

B. (9) General description of sighting
In answer to this question it is hoped to obtain a general description of what the observer actually saw and the circumstances under which he observed it.

B. (12) Position in which first seen
The position of the object seen may be described conveniently by bearing and elevation. By **bearing** it is meant the direction from the observer towards the object in terms of the cardinal points of the compass, or if possible, more accurately in the terms of degrees East or West of true North. It is useful to give the direction from the observer to the object in relation to the roads or concession lines. The level horizon is taken as zero degrees, the point directly overhead is 90 degrees.

B. (13) Position in which last seen
Note: See remarks under B. (12). This description should be as full and complete as possible. If there was any change in shape during the course of the observation, such change in shape should be indicated. The average man's left hand, with arm fully stretched out gives the following measurements.

(a) Between the first and second knuckles   3°
(b) Across the knuckles   8°
(c) With fingers extended, from point of index
    finger to point of little finger   12°
(d) With fingers extended from tip of thumb
    to tip of little finger   19°

Note: See Fig. (1) at top of page 163.

Because of the distance from the observer, the three dimensional form cannot generally be determined. However, the object will have an apparent shape in two dimensions, circular, oval, rectangular, triangular, etc. The two dimensional shape of the outline should be reported, not as an assumed three dimensional form.

B. (16) Detailed description of apparent brightness
It is realized that a description of apparent brightness is extremely difficult. However, if the object is seen at night or after

sundown it might be compared to the brightness of the moon, planets or stars.

B. (17) **Detailed description of colour**
In describing colour the simplest terms possible should be used such as red, green, white, etc.

B. (18) **Apparent size (angle subtended)**
The same technique for determining the apparent size of the object could be used as under B. (12) for determining its elevation. For information purposes the full moon subtends an angle of approximately ½ degree which is the angle subtended by a ¼ inch object held at arm's length. Since it is quite impossible to form even a rudimentary estimate of the size in feet or inches unless the distance is known, the size should be stipulated only in terms of the angle subtended by the object as seen by the observer.

B. (24) **Other contributory evidence (photographic, electronic, etc.)**
An effort should be made to uncover any evidence of a photographic, electronic, magnetic or radioactive nature which might have some association with the sighting. No unusual happenings at the time or place of sighting should be overlooked.

B. (25) **Any other details**
Under this heading a sketch of the path would be extremely helpful. This need only be a line drawing showing the position and orientation of the object in relation to visible land marks. If the observer should happen to be close enough to the object to form an opinion as to its shape and construction, a sketch to an approximate scale would be extremely valuable.

C. (27) **Date and place of interrogation**
An interview which takes place at the point from which the observer saw the object is the most valuable, since position bearings, elevation, etc., may be established more accurately in this way. It should be specified if the interview was conducted at the observation point.

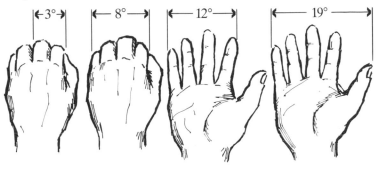

Figure 1

PROJECT SECOND STOREY

Part II——Descriptions of Normal Phenomena which might cause reports of unidentified aerial objects.

Balloons

Ceiling Balloons and unlighted Pilot Balloons are used in daytime. These balloons are about two feet in diameter. Red or White colours are employed.

At night, pilot balloons carry either a paper lantern lighted by a candle or a small battery-powered electric light. These are not likely to be visible to any great height by the naked eye, but a balloon with a slow leak might carry a light across the sky for a considerable distance at a relatively low level.

Radiosonde balloons are about five or six feet in diameter, coloured white, and carry a small box at the end of a cord about twenty feet below the balloon. Sometimes a radar reflector is also tied to the balloon; this is a reflector of many faces and it is possible that some unusual reflections of light may occur from this attachment. Radiosonde balloons normally ascend to about 60,000 feet.

Skyhook Balloons are used occasionally for special high-altitude observations which takes them up to 100,000 feet. These balloons are about 75 feet in diameter and an instrument box tied beneath. Because of their size, there is a good possibility that

163

such balloons are the basis of some reports of unusual aerial objects.

In the daytime with blue skies, good visibility and bright sunshine, balloons may be seen at considerable heights once they are located by the eye. The balloons stand out against the blue of the sky as sharp pin points of light.

Aircraft

Aircraft seen in this country should conform to the well known silhouettes but, in view of developments in neighbouring countries, triangular (delta wing) and tailless types, possibly flying at great heights, may be seen. Also due to distances and aircraft attitudes in flight, the true plan forms may not be observed. A change in shape during the observation may well indicate the existence of these circumstances.

Effects of Screens, Glass, Etc.

Common objects when viewed through screens may be distorted out of all recognizable shapes; often single objects may appear as several. As commercial sheet glass (window panes) may contain defects causing similar optical phenomena, observers should be wary of such conditions.

Nacreous or Mother of Pearl Clouds

These rare clouds are most likely to be seen just before sunrise or just after sunset when illuminated by sunshine from below the horizon. They may also appear in daytime. The clouds occur at heights of 15 to 20 miles and have iridescent colours which resemble the colours seen in mother of pearl. It is possible that a small detached mother of pearl cloud might give the appearance of a hovering object high in the sky.

Noctilucent Clouds

Noctilucent or night-luminous clouds are seen only at night made visible by reflected light from the sun when the sun is about 10° to 18° below the horizon and visibility conditions are very good. They usually appear about an hour after sunset, low on the horizon. Their colour may be white or they may be a shade of colour such as bluish-white, golden, or reddish-orange, but they do not display the brilliant iridescent colours that are characteristic of mother of pearl clouds. Noctilucent clouds occur about 50 miles high in the atmosphere, as determined by simultaneous photography from different points on the earth's surface. Their speeds have been calculated to be as high as 400 miles per hour, but because of their great height they appear to move slowly.

Clouds Reflections

Reflections of light from cloud banks are also a possible source of reports of illuminated objects in the sky at night. The source of light may be any kind of a searchlight, such as ceiling projectors, defence units, aircraft landing-lights, etc. Usually a beam of the light is visible from the source up to illuminated spot, so this condition is not likely to deceive a careful observer.

Optical Phenomena

Rainbows are common optical phenomena caused by a refraction and reflection of light from the sun by water drops in the atmosphere. A small portion only of a rainbow may be seen at times which might give the appearance of a small object in the sky. However, because rainbows are fairly common occurence, they are unlikely to deceive anyone.

Optical phenomena caused by reflections of light from ice crystals suspended in the atmosphere may result in the appearance of unusual lighting effects in the sky. The **halo** around the sun or moon is the most common of this class of phenomena. The halo is usually seen as a ring of 22° radius around the sun or moon, but under some conditions it is possible for only part of the ring to be formed. **Sundogs** or **mock-suns** may appear at an angle of 22° either to the right or left of the sun—these appear as bright spots of light in the sky. Mock-suns sometimes are seen at angles of 46° or 90° from the sun. The possibility of halo phenomena should always be considered when any bright spot is seen in the sky—such spots will remain relatively fixed in position. Halo phenomena are most commonly caused by the sun because of the large amount of light available from this source, but the complete halo ring is frequently seen around the moon at night and it is possible that under unusual conditions other halo phenomena may also be seen at night.

Meteors

A meteor, or shooting star, always pursues a nearly straight (or great circle) path across the sky. Faint meteors last about half a second, brighter ones rarely more than two or three seconds. Bright meteors may burst and shower sparks or may leave a faint luminescence in their wake that is sometime visible for several minutes. Bright meteors may appear of almost any colour and in exceptional cases produce detonations and rumbling sounds. When coming head on a meteor seems to have almost no motion across the sky but when moving perpendicular to the line of sight its apparent velocity is rapid.

Stars and Planets

Stars and planets can generally be recognized without difficulty but on certain occasions appear with unusual brilliance thus exciting comment. In any case they never move rapidly but have a slow general motion from the east to the west part of the sky, except for the stars in the north where the motion is counter-clockwise about the pole star. Venus at its greatest brilliance can appear in the sunlit-sky as a faint white dot visible to the naked eye. It either precedes or follows the sun on these occasions.

The Aurora

The aurora, or northern light, produces various luminous forms of numerous pastel shades. In most parts of Canada northern lights may appear in any part of the sky though they are seen most frequently in the north. Although sharp rays may appear as part of the display most of the illumination is of a very diffuse type and is subject to rapid motion and change of intensity reminding one of the great flickering flames or searchlight playing over clouds. Sometimes small, restricted auroral glows remain almost stationary in one place for some period of time. In general outlines are diffuse.

166

PROJECT SECOND STOREY
Sighting Report*

(A Separate form is to be used for each observer).

A. Details of observer.
   1. Name of observer:
   2. Address of observer:
   3. Occupation and previous relevant experience:
   4. Age Group:
   5. Has observer seen "flying objects" before, and if so, briefly, when, where, and circumstances:
   6. Was observer wearing glasses?

B. Details of Observation.
   7. Date and local time:
   8. Position of observer as accurately as possible:
   9. General description of sighting:
   10. Number of objects:
   11. Length of time observed:
   12. Position in which first seen:
       Bearing:
       Elevation:
   13. Position in which last seen:
       Bearing:
       Elevation:
   14. General description of any changes in the direction of motion.
   15. Detailed description of apparent shape:
   16. Detailed description of apparent brightness:
   17. Detailed description of color.
   18. Apparent size (e.g. angle subtended):
   19. Description of exhaust or vapour trails, if any:
   20. Description of noise, if any:
   21. Weather conditions:
       (a) Clouds:
       (b) Visibility:
       (c) Precipitation:
       (d) General remarks:
   22. Was the object flying above, below or in and out of cloud?
   23. Did anyone else see the object? If so, names and addresses:
   24. Is there other contributory evidence:
       (Photographic, or electronic, etc.)
   25. Any other details: (including sketch if possible):

C. Details of Interrogator:
   26. Interrogator:
      Surname:
      Initials:
      Position held:
   27. Date and place of interrogation:
   28. Interrogator's opinion of the reliability of the observer.

(Signature of Interrogator)

* The generous spacing provided in the actual report form under each question for insertion of the answers has been eliminated here for the purpose of reducing space.

WEIGHTING FACTORS FOR ANALYSIS OF SIGHTING REPORTS

In the analysis of sighting reports it is fairly obvious that different reports will have widely different values from the viewpoint of reliability, confirmation and lucidity. A formula has been devised giving approximately the same significance to each of these factors and derived from numerical values assigned to the answers given to the various questions on the Project Second Storey sighting report form.

The formula is as follows:—weight equals the cube root of the product of the reliability, confirmation and lucidity factors each expressed as decimals.

To facilitate obtaining numerical values for each of the factors, a scheme has been worked out for assigning points to each question such that for each factor the maximum possible score would be 100%. An equalizing scheme has been included so as to reduce to a minimum the opinion or judgment of the person assigning the score. It is expected that in this manner reasonably consistent scores will be obtained from which the various factors may be determined and a fair overall weighting factor calculated.

It should be noted that the cube root feature of the weighting factor minimizes the effect of any one particular aspect of the report and allows better assessment on the overall report.

In the following paragraphs reference is to the Project Second Storey sighting report form, Appendix I.

RELIABILITY:

Under Reliability the following maximum points have been assigned.

Question 3—15 points	Question 6 —5 points
Question 4—5 points	Question 27—20 points
Question 5—5 points	Question 28—50 points

In assigning points for Question 3 a trained observer in sky work should rate between 10 and 15, a trained observer in other fields should rate between 5 and 10 and an untrained observer should rate between 0 and 5. With reference to age, Question 4, if the observer is over 21 but under 65 years a maximum of 5 points; 18 to 21, 4 points; 15 to 18, 3 points; 12 to 15, 2 points; 9 to 12, 1 point, less than 9, 0 points. Over 65 but under 70 years, 4 points; 70 to 75, 3 points; 75 to 80, 2 points; 80 to 85, 1 point; over 85, 0 points.

Question number 5, no flying objects seen previously or if so such objects were completely recognized, 5 points; unidentified objects seen occasionally 2-4 points; unidentified objects frequently seen 0-2.

Question number 6, no glasses, 5 points; glasses normally worn and worn at the time of sighting, 4 points, bi-focal glasses normally worn and used at the time of sighting, 3 points; two kinds of glasses normally worn with wrong kind on at time of sighting, 2 points; glasses normally worn but not used at time of sighting, 0 to 1 point.

CONFIRMATION:

In the confirmation factor answers to Questions 21, 23 and 24 are essentially confirmatory. A fixed score of 50% is accorded because of the fact that the sighting was reported by this one observer. If the weather conditions covered by Question 21 are confirmed completely or partially by official weather reports a score of up to 10 points may be allowed. If the sighting was also witnessed by other people a score of up to 30 points may be allowed, distributed as follows: 2 other witnesses unknown to each other and geographically separated, 25 to 30 points; one other witness as above 20 to 25 points; more than one witness at the same place and time, 15 to 20 points; witnesses elsewhere with some factors, such as direction, time, etc. in doubt, 10 to 15 points; other witnesses of doubtful confirmation 5 to 10 points; vague or no confirmation, 0 to 5 points. Up to 10 points should be allowed for confirmation by other means as in Question 24.

LUCIDITY:

The lucidity factor should be considered as completely independent of reliability or confirmation and should deal only with the value of the information given, assuming that it is completely reliable and entirely confirmed. In assigning scores to the various questions extreme care should be used to avoid influencing the

170

score by any prejudice regarding reliability or confirmation as these two factors are taken care of adequately in the overall formula for obtaining the weighting factor.

Question 8—if the position of the observer can be plotted as a pencil point on a map, scale one mile to one inch, 5 points should be allowed; if the position can be established within one city block or a square 500' on the side, 4 points should be allowed; within a square 2000' on the side, 3 points should be allowed; within one square mile, 2 points should be allowed; within city or township limits, one point should be allowed; general area only, zero points.

If a specific description of the sighting is given 8 to 10 points may be allowed. If a good analogy is given 6 to 8 points may be allowed. A poor analogy given 4 to 6 points may be allowed. A vague description 2 to 4 points may be allowed. Where the number of objects seen is specifically stated, 2 points may be given to be reduced towards zero if there is any doubt.

In Question 11, the length of time during which the sighting was observed and the degree of accuracy which appears to be indicated should be used to determine a score from 5 down to zero.

In Questions 12 and 13, if the bearing and elevation can be established within plus or minus 5°, 5 points each should be allowed for bearing and elevation. If the determination is between 5° and 10°, 4 points should be allowed; if between 10° and 20°, 3 points should be allowed; if between 20° and 45°, 2 points should be allowed; if general directions only are given, one point, if no or unsatisfactory information is given, zero points. If a statement is given regarding the change in course, 2 points should be accorded; if the statement is vague only 1 point; or if information is not given, zero.

Under Question 15, if a definite shape was apparent and described specifically, 5 points; if the shape was poorly described, 4 points; if the shape was indefinite, 3 points; if it was a blur or spot of light, 2 points; any vague description, 1 point; no information, zero.

With respect to colour, if the description is such that the colour can be identified on a spectrum chart 5 points may be allowed; if it is compared with some common light source 4 points may be allowed; if it is referred to an equivalent temperature three points may be allowed; if a general description only is given 2 points; an indefinite statement 1 point; no information, zero.

With respect to size, if the angle subtended was determined at the time of the sighting and can be specified within 10% 8 to 10 points may be allowed; if the angle was determined after the sighting and it is estimated to be within 10%, 6 to 8 points; if the angle is referred to the angle subtended by the sun or full moon, 4 to 6 points; if the angle is referred to the angle subtended by a familiar object at a stated distance, 2 to 4 points; vague description only, zero to 2.

If exhaust or vapour trails are indicated or statement as to their absence 2 points may be allowed; if there is any degree of doubt the score should be reduced towards zero.

Answers concerning noise should be given 3 points if they are specific and reduced towards zero if they are not specific.

Under weather conditions the total possible score of 5 should be scaled in proportion to the number of statements confirmed by official weather report.

Question 22, if a specific statement was made concerning the position of the object with reference to clouds 2 points may be allowed; scaled down towards zero if there is any doubt.

Under Question 25, if details are consistently described, 20 to 25 points; if details are loosely described 15 to 20 points, if they are vaguely described, 10 to 15 points; if details are absent and general description only is given, 5 to 10 points, and if a vague general description only is given, zero to 5 points.

Under Question 27, if the interview took place at the site of the sighting at a similar time and day and within a week, 20 points may be accorded; if the interview was at the site at a similar time of day and later than a week, 15 to 20 points; if at the site at a different time of day, 15 points, if not at the site but within a week, 10 to 15 points; not at the site and/or later than a week, zero to 10 points.

Under Question 28, is the interrogator's opinion of the reliability of the observer. Answers to questions 3, 4, 5, 6, and 27 should go a long way towards establishing the reliability of the observer and the score obtained from the answers to these five questions should form the guide for the score to be assigned to Question 28. If, however, the interrogator's opinion appears to indicate a substantial deviation from the total so obtained the score for Question 28 should be adjusted accordingly. The maximum score possible is 50 and under normal circumstances should be about the same as the total score for questions 3, 4, 5, 6 and 27.

APPENDIX III

SAUCER SIGHTING ANALYSIS CHARTS

174

Chart I

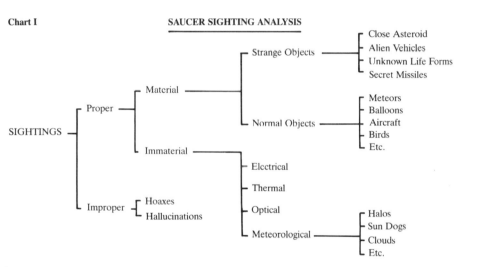

SIGHTINGS

Proper
  Material
    Strange Objects
      Close Asteroid
      Alien Vehicles
      Unknown Life Forms
      Secret Missiles
    Normal Objects
      Meteors
      Balloons
      Aircraft
      Birds
      Etc.
  Immaterial
    Electrical
    Thermal
    Optical
    Meteorological
      Halos
      Sun Dogs
      Clouds
      Etc.

Improper
  Hoaxes
  Hallucinations

175

Chart II　　　　**SAUCER SIGHTING ANALYSIS**

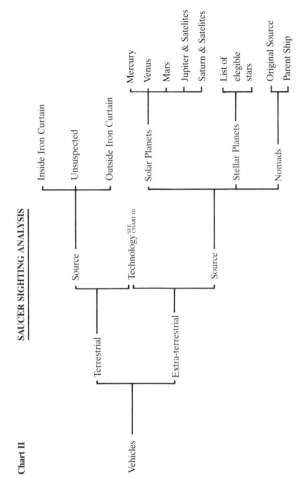

- Vehicles
  - Terrestrial
    - Source
      - Inside Iron Curtain
      - Unsuspected
      - Outside Iron Curtain
  - Extra-terrestrial
    - Technology SEE CHART III
    - Source
      - Solar Planets
        - Mercury
        - Venus
        - Mars
        - Jupiter & Satelites
        - Saturn & Satelites
      - Stellar Planets
        - List of elegible stars
      - Nomads
        - Original Source
        - Parent Ship

Chart III

SAUCER SIGHTING ANALYSIS

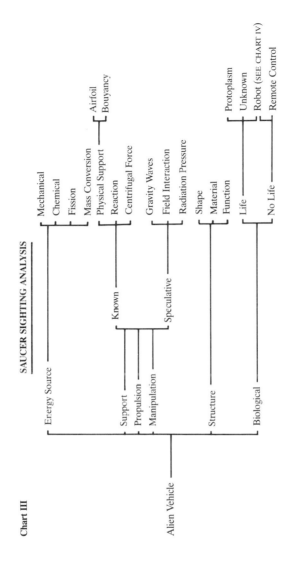

Alien Vehicle

- Energy Source
  - Mechanical
  - Chemical
  - Fission
  - Mass Conversion
- Support
  - Known
    - Physical Support
      - Airfoil
      - Bouyancy
    - Reaction
    - Centrifugal Force
- Propulsion
- Manipulation
  - Speculative
    - Gravity Waves
    - Field Interaction
    - Radiation Pressure
- Structure
  - Shape
  - Material
  - Function
- Biological
  - Life
    - Protoplasm
    - Unknown
    - Robot (SEE CHART IV)
  - No Life
    - Remote Control

Chart IV   <u>**SAUCER SIGHTING ANALYSIS**</u>

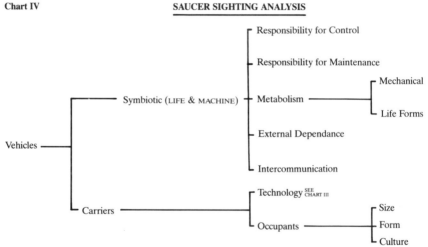

Chart V

SAUCER SIGHTING ANALYSIS

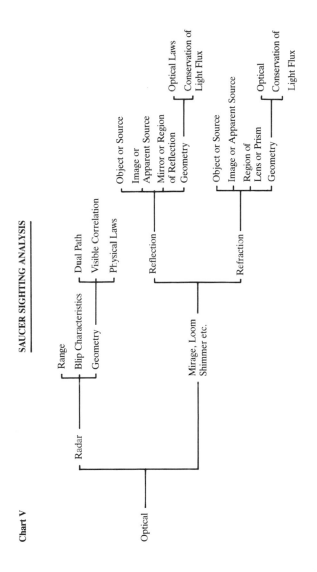

179

Chart VI

SAUCER SIGHTING ANALYSIS

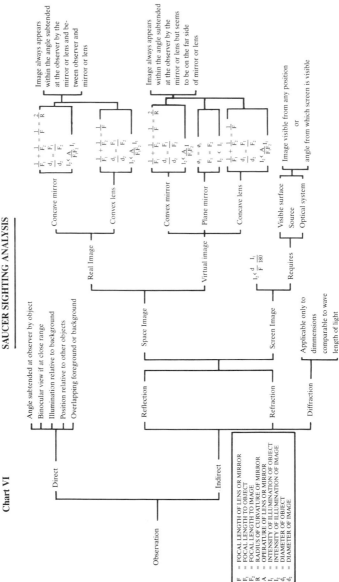

Observation

— **Direct**
- Angle subtended at observer by object
- Binocular view if at close range
- Illumination relative to background
- Position relative to other objects
- Overlapping foreground or background

— **Indirect**
- Reflection
- Refraction
- Diffraction — Applicable only to dimensions comparable to wave length of light

Reflection / Refraction → Space Image

Space Image → Real Image

- **Concave mirror**
$$\frac{1}{F_1} + \frac{1}{F_2} = \frac{1}{F} = \frac{2}{R}$$
$$\frac{d_i}{d_o} = \frac{F_2}{F_1}$$
$$I_2 < \frac{A}{F_1 F_2} I_1$$

- **Convex lens**
$$\frac{1}{F_1} + \frac{1}{F_2} = \frac{1}{F}$$
$$\frac{d_i}{d_o} = \frac{F_2}{F_1}$$
$$I_2 < \frac{A}{F_1 F_2} I_1$$

> Image always appears within the angle subtended at the observer by the mirror or lens and between observer and mirror or lens

Space Image → Virtual image

- **Convex mirror**
$$\frac{1}{F_1} + \frac{1}{F_2} = \frac{1}{F} = \frac{2}{R}$$
$$\frac{d_i}{d_o} = \frac{F_2}{F_1}$$
$$I_2 < \frac{A}{F_1 F_2} I_1$$

- **Plane mirror**
$$\theta_1 = \theta_2$$
$$F_1 = F_2$$
$$I_2 < I_1$$

- **Concave lens**
$$\frac{1}{F_1} + \frac{1}{F_2} = \frac{1}{F}$$
$$\frac{d_i}{d_o} = \frac{F_2}{F_1}$$
$$I_2 < \frac{A}{F_1 F_2} I_1$$

> Image always appears within the angle subtended at the observer by the mirror or lens but seems to be on the far side of mirror or lens

Refraction → Screen Image

$$I_2 < \frac{d}{F} \frac{I_1}{180}$$

Requires:
- Visible surface
- Source
- Optical system

> Image visible from any position
> or
> angle from which screen is visible

F = FOCAL LENGTH OF LENS OR MIRROR
F_1 = FOCAL LENGTH TO OBJECT
F_2 = FOCAL LENGTH TO IMAGE
R = RADIUS OF CURVATURE OF MIRROR
A = OPERATURE OF LENS OR MIRROR
I_1 = INTENSITY OF ILLUMINATION OF OBJECT
I_2 = INTENSITY OF ILLUMINATION OF IMAGE
d_o = DIAMETER OF OBJECT
d_i = DIAMETER OF IMAGE

Chart VII

SAUCER SIGHTING ANALYSIS

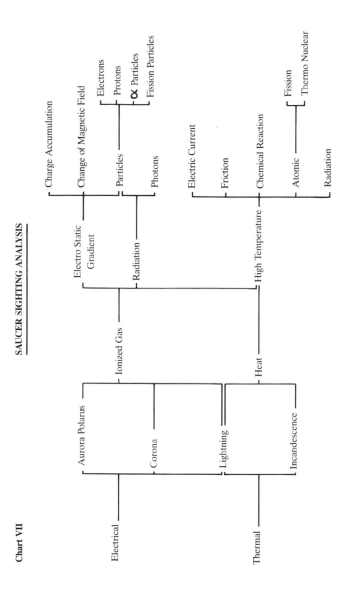

Chart VIII   SAUCER SIGHTING ANALYSIS

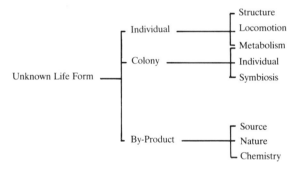

Chart IX   <u>SAUCER SIGHTING ANALYSIS</u>

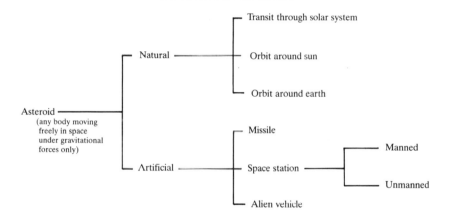

APPENDIX IV

Summary of Sightings Reported to and Analysed by

Department of Transport During 1952.

Following is a summary of the sightings investigated by the Department of Transport during 1952. A few other sightings were reported but were obviously of conventional objects and are omitted from this analysis. These summary reports are much abbreviated but contain the salient features. The names of the observers have been omitted since many of them were reluctant to have their names used and consented to give the information requested only on the distinct understanding that their names would not be quoted. The names, however, do appear on the sighting report forms or other official documents.

No evaluations of the individual sightings are included in these summaries, although in some cases the nature of the observed object is fairly obvious. In other cases the evaluations required much research and lengthy calculations, in trying to make them fit the various theories so far advanced. Most of these efforts were quite unsuccessful because the data lies outside conventional patterns.

The weighting factors shown have been worked out from the original data along the lines of Appendix II, and where more than one observer was involved, the respective weighting factors were combined according to Peter's Formula. These weighting factors are essentially the probability that the reports are reliable in themselves.

CASE 1, OTTAWA, MAY 1st, 1952, Weight 90%

At approximately 9.30 PM E.D.T. on May 1st a roundish, bright light streaked across Ottawa's southern horizon. It was seen by 6 people located in Ottawa and Aylmer who were interviewed immediately after the sighting. The light was visible about 12 seconds and went out abruptly at the end of its travel. Triangulations from data supplied by the observers fixed the termination of the path about over the Shirley Bay rifle range, with the start of the path somewhere near Uplands Airport. The altitude was computed at about 12,000 feet, and its speed at about 3,600 miles per hour. The path was estimated to be curved with the center of curvature near down town Ottawa. Triangulation computations estimated the diameter of the illuminated area as about 400 feet. The color of the light was predominately white, and it was very steady and the entire area appeared to be uniformly illuminated. The light suddenly went out at the end of its travel and nothing further was seen. There were no sounds reported.

Just preceding the above sighting two other observers noticed an orange ellipse in the south east sky from Ottawa, which appeared to hover for some time, after which it suddenly vanished. The closest estimate of time in this case places the sighting as occupying a half hour between 8.45 and 9.15 E.D.T. The planet Mars was in the sky at the time but at a somewhat different bearing and elevation claimed for the object. No special note was taken of the planet.

At approximately 9.15 PM E.D.T. a light was seen by a single observer in Smiths Falls moving rapidly from east to west across the south west sky. The general description of this light was similar to that seen from the Ottawa area, except that it appeared to subtend a smaller angle.

CASE II, KARS, ONTARIO, MAY 24, 1952, Weight 61%

Within a few minutes of 9.26 PM, E.D.T. a farmer near Kars noticed a dull red round object moving from west to north in the sky. It was in view about a minute and then vanished beyond the horizon. It appeared to be about two thirds the diameter of the full moon, but not as bright as that body. No sounds were heard.

CASE III, HALIFAX, N.S., MAY 26, 1952, Weight 81%

At about 10.35 PM, A.S.T., a brilliant blue light streaked from south to northeast across the Halifax sky, leaving a trail behind it. This was seen by observers in Spryfield, Bass River and River John by four separate people. Triangulation fixes the path as starting a little to the east of Halifax and terminating about over Tatamagouche. The duration of the sighting was about 2 seconds. The observer at River John claimed to have heard a hissing sound.

185

CASE IV, WENDOVER, ONTARIO, JUNE 6, 1952, Weight 64%

Five people in a car approaching Wendover at about 3.30 AM, E.D.T., noticed an orange red object moving from west north west to west, about 5° above the horizon, which was in view about a minute and then dropped below the horizon. The car was moving at the time.

CASE V, CALGARY, ALBERTA, JUNE 8, 1952, Weight 62%

A meteorological assistant was taking a Pibal observation at 11.47 AM, M.S.T., when a silvery ellipse, aspect ratio 8:1, crossed the field of vision of the theodolite. It was in view for 3 seconds. With reference to the height of the pibal balloon at the time the object was estimated to be higher than 50,000 feet. The object appeared to have a sharp outline and to shine from reflected sunlight.

CASE VI, HALIFAX, N.S., JUNE 15, 1952, Weight 75%

On June 15 at 8.32 AM, A.S.T., a meteorological assistant on reserve army manoeuvers noticed what seemed to be a large silver disc in the sky south east of Halifax. It moved southwest for about 30 seconds at an estimated altitude of 5,000 to 8,000 feet and then ascended vertically and in 2 to 5 seconds merged in altocumulus clouds at 11,000 to 12,000 feet. If the altitude estimates are correct, from the bearing and elevation data obtained from this observer, the diameter of the disc works out at about 100 feet. A large standard aircraft was also in the sky at the time and the object seemed to move much more rapidly than the plane. The object's speed was estimated to be at least 800 miles per hour.

CASE VII, OTTAWA, ONTARIO, JUNE 20, 1952, Weight 86%

Five people saw a brilliant object travel rapidly from south to north across the eastern sky from Ottawa at 9.48 PM, E.D.T. The sighting lasted about 4 seconds, and consisted of a brilliant irregularly shaped head followed by a short luminous tail. Triangulation placed the path between 50 and 100 miles east of Ottawa, and from south to north.

CASE VIII, PECKSFORDS ISLAND, NFLD., JUNE 27, 1952, Weight 71%

Two lightkeepers at the Peckfords Island lighthouse noticed at 12.35 AM Nfld. time a reddish light slightly above the horizon travelling slowly from south to north east. Both lightkeepers ascertained that there was no boat or other object associated with the light.

CASE IX, VANCOUVER, B.C., JULY 3, 1952, Weight 39%

A single observer noticed at 11.55 PM, P.D.T., a bright round amber light move from the south in a northwesterly direction, until it was about due west when it turned and headed southwest. The object was in view about 1 minute.

CASE X, OTTAWA, ONTARIO, JULY 8, 1952, Weight 69%

A commissionaire on duty at an army depot saw a bright light about one quarter the size of the full moon, light orange in color, which travelled from the south towards the north, turned and travelled south again. It was in view about 1 minute. The time was about 10.15 PM, E.D.T.

CASE XI, BELLS CORNERS, ONTARIO, JULY 17, 1952, Weight 66%

On July 17 at about 10.50 PM, E.D.T., an observer in a car on Highway 15 near Bells Corners noticed a bright flash in the south east sky which consisted of a bright cream coloured object which travelled towards the south, broke into pieces and left a white trail which persisted for about 15 seconds.

CASE XII, HALIFAX, N.S., JULY 18, 1952, Weight 68%

At approximately midnight A.S.T. on July 18, an ex-airforce officer noticed a gold coloured bright ring about some central object which travelled rapidly from the north west towards the east and disappeared below the horizon. The angle subtended was about one quarter size of the full moon, and was visible about 8 or 9 seconds. There was no sound reported and no trails.

CASE XIII, OTTAWA, ONTARIO, JULY 20, 1952, Weight 74%

At approximately 11.42 AM, E.D.T. a tear drop shaped object was seen by a single observer for about 4 seconds as it flew into a cloud. The object was described as very shiny bright and about one eighth size of the full moon. The course covered an arc of about 50° at an elevation of about 30° to 40°, and appeared to be curving towards its left.

CASE XIV, OTTAWA, ONTARIO, JULY 25, 1952, Weight 74%

At about 8.00 AM, E.D.T., seven bright objects were seen in V formation in the west and travelling south. They appeared bright, bluish and self luminous, round and about one half size of the moon. Again at about 11.45 AM, E.D.T., two more similar objects were seen north and travelling south east.

CASE XV, CARAQUET, N.B., JULY 30, 1952, Weight 53%

Between 6 and 7 PM, A.S.T., July 30, the lightkeeper at Caraquet observed a brilliantly shiny cone shaped object about 45° above the horizon, travelling from south to east.

CASE XVI, NOOTKA, B.C., JULY 30, 1952, Weight 68%

On July 30, 1952, at 1.37 AM, P.S.T. the lightkeeper at Nootka Station observed a luminous object travelling northwest by north. It was in view between 3 and 4 seconds and passed almost overhead. There was no sound or vapour trail.

CASE XVII, MACDONALD, MANITOBA, AUGUST 27, 1952, Weight 73%

A disc shaped object with shadows on it as if it had an irregular surface was seen by two meteorological officers at 4.45 AM, C.S.T. at MacDonald Airport. It was well below the altocumulus clouds at 5,000 feet, and subtended an angle of about 3° and was about 30° above the horizon, and apparently right over the airport. The object made two turns about the field and when struck by the light from the rotating beacon made off toward the northeast and was out of sight within a second. There was no sound whatsoever. The object glinted like shiny aluminum when the beacon light struck it.

CASE XVIII, ALERT, N.W.T., NOVEMBER 25, 1952, Weight 55%

A meteorological observer at Alert, N.W.T., observed a lighted area in the sky which persisted for about 2 seconds, at

8.32 AM, G.M.T. The sky was overcast with a ceiling of about 2,000 feet. Lightning is practically unknown at these latitudes and there are no beacons within several hundred miles of Alert.

CASE XIX, REGINA, SASK., DECEMBER 1, 1952, Weight 68%

A number of school children on their way home observed two bright star-like objects overhead with cloudlike tails travelling from north to south at 11.45 AM, M.S.T. The motion was slow and regular with the two objects alternating in the lead. A meteorologist employed by the Department of Transport, interviewed one of the children by telephone and was able to estimate the height of the objects as the same as the cirrus clouds present at the time. The meteorologist checked with the airport control tower and found that a single conventional aircraft was the only one in the vicinity.

CASE XX, PRINCE RUPERT, B.C., DECEMBER 3, 1952, Weight 68%

The Chief Officer of a Canadian Government Steamship at berth in Prince Rupert at 8.00 AM, P.S.T., on December 3 observed a small bright object travelling east from a position north of the observer. It was about the same brightness as a major planet and subtended about the same angle as Jupiter at its nearest approach to the Earth. It was in view about 6 seconds. There was no sound and no trail.

CASE XXI, OTTAWA, ONTARIO, DECEMBER 16, 1952, Weight 68%

A bright disc shaped object subtending an angle of about 4' was observed at 5.14 PM, E.S.T., travelling very fast from north to south west. It was in view for 3½ seconds. The outline was sharp, and the major axis of the projected ellipse was always parallel to the horizon. The colour was similar to the planet Venus, but became slightly more reddish as it approached the horizon. There was no noise and no trail.

CASE XXII, WHITE RIVER, ONTARIO, DECEMBER 17, 1952

A railway yard employee observed a bright green flash in the south south west direction at 4.45 AM, E.S.T. There was no trail or sound.

CASE XXIII, REGINA, SASK., DECEMBER 27, 1952, Weight 74%

From 7.34 PM, M.S.T., to 7.42 PM, M.S.T., the airport control tower officer watched a round luminous object subtending an angle about one third that of the full moon, travel downwards and disappear beyond the horizon. It travelled a vertical angle of 5° in 1½ minutes. Object was viewed through 7x50 field glasses and a red flashing light on top and a green flashing light on the bottom were observed. Through the glasses the object appeared about the size of the full moon. There was no sound or trail.

CASE XXIV, REGINA, SASK., DECEMBER 31, 1952, Weight 78%

The Meteorological officer and Air Traffic controller at the Regina Airport observed a luminous circular object subtending about 8′, travelling downwards to disappear beyond the horizon at 3.10 AM, M.S.T. It travelled the first 5 degrees of its downward arc in 4 minutes and the last 5 degrees in three minutes. There was no additional detail visible through the field glasses.

CASE XXV, REGINA, SASK., DECEMBER 31, 1952, Weight 76%

Approximately 20 minutes after CASE XXIV at 3.30 AM, M.S.T., the same observers saw another somewhat similar object descending towards the horizon covering an arc of about 15 degrees in 3 or 4 minutes. This object seemed to fluctuate in brilliancy with about a 5 second period, appearing larger when brighter. The colour of the objects seen in CASES XXIII, XXIV, AND XXV was similar to that of a harvest moon, and about the same intensity. The objects definitely were not associated witH the only aircraft aloft at the times of the sightings.

ANNEX 5

REPORT ON DOT ACTIVITIES

Based on the conclusions of the 1952 report, it was felt that certain of the phenomenae would probably be accompanied by physical effects which could be measured, and since measurements are always more satisfactory than qualitative observations, it was decided to try and get some measured data.

Whether the phenomenae be due to natural electromagnetic causes, or alien vehicles, there would probably be associated with a sighting some magnetic or radio noise disturbance. Also, there is a possibility of gamma radiation being associated with such phenomenae.

It has been suggested by some mathematicians that gravity waves may exist in reality, as well as a convenience to make an equation balance. While we know practically nothing of such waves in nature, nevertheless, if the possibility exists, flying saucer phenomenae, being largely an unknown field, might be a good place to look for such gravity waves.

Therefore, a group of instruments was set up in a hut at Shirley Bay for the purpose of trying to get measurements which could be tied to one or more actual sightings. The instruments are: a compass type magnetometer, a gamma ray counter, a radio set and gravimeter. The outputs of these four instruments are arranged to draw proportional traces on a 4 pen recorder.

These instruments went into operation last October and apart from the usual bugs, seem to be operating satisfactorily. We have as yet obtained no saucer data from them.

Our future plans include study of any data which we may get from our Shirley Bay set-up, should we be so fortunate, as well as the continued analysis of sighting reports which come in to us. We propose also to make rigid analysis of known phenomenae to see how much can be explained on this basis. Most of the previous work along these lines has been largely qualitative and open to serious objection from the point of view of quantitative analysis.

191

We intend to promote a study of gravity waves, whether within this Department or outside to find out if:

a) They exist in nature
b) How we can detect them if they do
c) How to generate them, and
d) What they may be used for.

NOTES AND REFERENCES

CHAPTER 3

1. Montreal **Star,** March 22, 1978.

2. Hynek, J. Allen, **The Hynek UFO Report,** Dell, New York, 1977, p.8.

3. 1973 Gallup Poll as reported by Friedman, Stanton F. in "Flying Saucers and Physics", **Proceedings 1974 MUFON Symposium,** Mutual UFO Network, Seguin, Texas.

4. Former Professor of Astronomy, Northwestern University, Director of the Center for UFO Studies, and former scientific advisor on UFOs to the U.S. Air Force.

5. Hynek, J. Allen, **The UFO Experience: A Scientific Inquiry.** Henry Regnery, Chicago, 1972, pp 28-29.

6. Saunders, David R. "UFO Activity in Relation to Day of the Week", **Flying Saucer Review,** London, Vol. 17, No. 1, 1971.

7. Sturrock, P.A., **Report on a Survey of the Membership of the American Astronomical Society Concerning the UFO Problem,** SUIPR Report No. 681, Institute for Plasma Research, Stanford University, Stanford, 1977.

8. **Scientific Study of Unidentified Flying Objects,** E.P. Dutton, New York, 1969, pp 42, 176 - 209.

9. **Introductory Space Science,** Physics 370 Course Text, U.S. Air Force Academy, pp 462-3.

10. Fuller, John G., **The Interrupted Journey,** Dial Press, New York, 1966.

11. ibid.

12. Dickinson, Terrance, **The Zeta Reticuli Incident,** Astro Media Corp. Milwaukee, 1976.

13. Case No. DND120, NRC Non-Meteoric Sighting Files.

14. "UFO Occupants Seen Near Hospital", **Canadian UFO Report,** Duncan, B.C., Vol. 1, No. 7, Summer 1970.

15. Case No. N69/091, NRC Non-Meteoric Sighting Files.

16. Letter to Author from Dr. Bruce McIntosh dated April 30, 1969.

17. Cannon, Brian "Strange Case of Falcon Lake, Part I", **Canadian UFO Report,** Duncan, B.C., Vol. 1, No. 2, 1969.

18. Cannon, Part II, Vol. 1, No. 3, 1969.

19. Cannon, Part III, Vol. 1, No. 4, 1969.

20. House of Commons Debates (Hansard) February 6, 1969, p. 5236.

21. Case No. DND 200, NRC Non-Meteoric Sighting Files.

22. Ottawa **Citizen,** 11 December, 1973.

23. Wilson, Clifford, **UFOs and Their Mission Impossible,** New American Library of Canada, Toronto, 1975.

CHAPTER 4

1. Chant, C.A. "An Extraordinary Meteoric Display", **The Journal of the Royal Astronomical Society of Canada,** Vol. VII, No. 3., 1913.

2. ibid p. 149.

3. ibid p. 149.

4. ibid p. 151.

5. ibid p. 155.

6. Chant, C.A., "Further Information Regarding the Meteoric Display of February 9, 1913", **R.A.S.C. Journal,** Vol. VII, No. 6, 1913, p. 445.

7. Chant, **R.A.S.C. Journal,** Vol. VII, No. 3, 1913, pp. 158-9.

8. Chant, **R.A.S.C. Journal,** Vol. VII, No. 6, 1913, p. 447.

9. Chant, **R.A.S.C. Journal,** Vol. VII, No. 3, 1913, p. 158.

10. ibid, p. 162.

11. Denning, W.F. "Notes on the Great Meteoric Stream of 1913, February 9th, Seen in Canada and the United States", **R.A.S.C. Journal,** Vol. VII, No. 6, 1913, p. 404.

12. O'Keefe, John A. "New Data on Cyrillids", **R.A.S.C. Journal,** Vol. 62, No. 3, 1968, pp 97-98.

13. Davidson, M. "The American Meteor Display of February 9th, 1913", IN Chant, C.A., "Further Information Regarding the Meteoric Display of February 9, 1913", **R.A.S.C. Journal,** Vol. VII, No. 6, 1913, p. 441.

CHAPTER 5

1. Jacobs, David M., **The UFO Controversy in America,** Indiana University Press, Bloomington, 1975.

2. Bray, Arthur, **Science, the Public and the UFO,** Bray Book Service, Ottawa, 1967.

3. **Proceedings of the Special Senate Committee on Science Policy,** No. 30, Appendix 212, Queen's Printer, Ottawa, 1970.

4. Letter from External Affairs dated April 13, 1971.

5. Letter from Director of Research, Special Senate Committee on Science Policy, dated September 15, 1970.

6. "Statement on International Scientific aspects of the Problem of Unidentified Flying Objects", **Unidentified flying Objects: Greatest Scientific Problem of our Times,** Pittsburg Sub-Committee, NICAP, 1967.

7. Translation from the German **UFO-nachrichten,** November, 1970.

8. Hynek, J. Allen, **The UFO Experience,** Henry Regnery Company, Chicago, 1972, p.222, footnote.

9. Letter from Department of External Affairs dated April 13, 1971.

10. International UFO Reporter, Chicago, October 1976.

11. Stringfield, Leonard H., "Inside Look at Grenada's UFO Mission at the United Nations", **International UFO Reporter,** Chicago, February, 1978.

12. **International UFO Reporter,** January 1978.

13. **International UFO Reporter,** vol. 3, no. 8, August 1978.

14. **Summary Record of the 35th meeting Special Political Committee, U.N. General Assembly,** Thirty-Third Session, November 27, 1978.

15. U.N. Press Release GA/AH/1479 dated November 27, 1978.

16. **Report of Special Political Committee of the United Nations,** A/33/512, dated December 16, 1978.

17. **Provisional Verbatim Record of the 87th Meeting, United Nations General Assembly,** A/33/pv.87, January 17, 1979.

18. **S.B.I. Report,** Scientific Bureau of Investigation Inc., Staten Island, N.Y. vol. 1, no. 4, 1979, p.5.

CHAPTER 6

1. Case No. N74/078 in NRC files.

2. Letter from Transport Canada dated June 7, 1976.

3. Case No.N67/045 in NRC files.

4. Case No. N74/052 in NRC files.

5. Records Unit, Publications and Record Management Division, Department of Communications, Room 906, Journal Tower North.

6. File No. 5010-4.

7. "Air Services General" with the sub-subject "Space Research and

Satellites — General", and the title "Unidentified Flying Objects (including Outer Space Travel)".

8. Dated February 16, 1959.

9. Dated January 31, 1961.

10. Dated February 3, 1961.

11. Volume 4.

12. Identified as "file 22-2-29 which contains sighting reports" and "file 22-12-33 'Project Magnet' (the physics of the subject)".

13. File 22-12-33 now held under file number 6650-4.

14. File No. 22-2-29.

15. Letter from DOC dated March 31, 1978.

16. Letter from Chief of Information Services, Department of Transport, dated March 13, 1967.

17. Letter from Dr. John de Mercado, Department of Communications, dated September 10, 1979.

18. Letter from Dr. Millman dated November 17, 1950.

19. "Electronic Bloodhounds Track Down 'Sky Stones'", **Science Dimension,** National Research Council, May, 1972.

20. Room 2026, 100 Sussex Drive, Ottawa, Ontario.

21. Telephone # (613) 996-9345.

22. These index cards are filed by date of report, not by serial number, but the report files are filed by serial number.

23. Letter from Dr. A.G. McNamara dated April 18, 1978.

24. Identified as "Correspondence A—L" and "Correspondence M—Z".

25. Letter from Col. L.A. Bourgeois, Director of Information Services, DND dated June 24, 1968.

26. Letter from the Hon. James Richardson dated September 15, 1975.

27. ibid.

28. Letter from Dr. A.G. McNamara dated April 18, 1978.

29. Unclassified, 940-150 Box 829624 (AF); Confidential, 940-5 Box 829627 (AF); Secret, 940-105-3 Box 829628 (AF); Secret, 9150-4 (1963TS) Army.

30. Letter from Directorate of History, DND, dated July 6, 1976.

31. Files viewed at Directorate of History were: 940-105, 940-105 vol. 2, 940-5 vol. 1, 940-105-3.

32. File No. 9150-4 (1963TS Army).

33. Magor, John, **Our UFO Visitors,** Hancock House Publishers, Saanichton, B.C., 1977, p. 74.

34. Letter from Col. L.A. Bourgeois dated June 24, 1968.

35. I already knew the answer to my question, but I wanted the government to spell it out.

36. Letter from Dr. A.G. McNamara dated February 4, 1974.

37. Letter from Hon. John Munro, dated March 22, 1974.

38. Letter from Department of External Affairs dated April 13, 1971.

39. **Examination of Samples from Metallic Material from Les Ecureuils, Quebec,** Dept. of Energy, Mines and Resources, Mines Branch Investigation Report 1R 71-32, Ottawa, May 7, 1971.

CHAPTER 7

1. Statement for delivery by Minister of Transport in House of Commons (undated) contained in file 5010-4 of Department of Communications (DOC) (former DOT file). (Annex 2).

2. House of Commons Debates (Hansard) December 4, 1963, p.5408, Question No. 1,416.

3. Letter to author from DOT dated November 20, 1964, (copy in DOC file 5010-4).

4. Letter from Dr. William D. Howe, MP, to J. R. Baldwin, Deputy Minister of Transport, dated April 7, 1966, (in DOC file 5010-4).

5. "Note on Project Magnet Report", dated May 9, 1968.

6. Letter in NRC file "Correspondence A to L" addressed to an enquirer dated September 24, 1968.

7. Smith, W. B. "Project Magnet: The Canadian Flying Saucer Study," **Topside,** Ottawa Flying Saucer Club, No. 12, 1963.

8. Smith, W. B. **Interim Report Project Magnet,** dated June 25, 1952 (Annex 3).

9. Smith, W. B. **Project Magnet Report,** (Annex 4).

10. Toronto **Daily Star,** November 14, 1953.

11. Letter from Dr. P. M. Millman dated September 24, 1968, in NRC files.

12. Form letter signed by Controller of Telecommunications, DOT, dated August 10, 1954.

13. **Topside,** Ottawa Flying Saucer Club, No. 12, 1963.

14. Memo from G. C. W. Browne to Supt. of Radio Regulations, dated June 25, 1954 in DOC file 5010-4.

15. Minutes of Second Meeting, Second Storey Committee, held May 19, 1952.

16. Reclassified "Open" on April 10, 1968.

17. Minutes of First Meeting, Second Storey Committee, held April 24, 1952.

18. At 2152 hours (9.52 p.m.) EST on September 8, 1952.

19. Minutes of Fourth Meeting, Second Storey Committee, held November 17, 1952.

20. Appendix to Minutes of Fourth Meeting, Second Storey Committee, held November 17, 1952.

21. Minutes of Fifth Meeting, Second Storey Committee, held March 9, 1953.

22. Letter from Dr. A. G. McNamara dated July 25, 1979.

23. Memo signed by Dr. Peter M. Millman dated November 21, 1953.

24. Leslie and Adamski, **Flying Saucers Have Landed,** T. Werner Laurie Ltd., London, 1953.

25. **Topside,** No. 12, 1963.

26. Writing executed without the agent's volition, and sometimes without his knowledge. The term is used by psychical researchers and applied particularly to the trance phenomena. On the other hand, automatic writing may be executed while the agent is in a condition scarcely varying from the normal and quite capable of observing the phenomena in a critical spirit, though perhaps ignorant of a word in advance of what he is actually writing.

27. Emenegger, Robert, **UFOs Past, Present and Future,** Ballantine Books, New York, 1974, pp. 58-62.

28. Jacobs, David M., **The UFO Controversy in America,** Indiana University Press, 1975, pp. 173-74.

29. Hynek, J. Allen, **The Hynek UFO Report,** Dell, New York, 1977, p. 7.

30. Smith, W. B., Submission to Director, Civil Aviation, undated.

31. Smith, W. B., "Binding Forces", **Topside,** Ottawa, No. 12, 1963.

32. Edwards, Frank, **Flying Saucers — Serious Business,** Bantam Books, New York, 1966, pp. 49-50.

33. House of Commons Special Committee on Broadcasting. Minutes of Proceedings and Evidence, No. 8. Tuesday May 17, 1955, Queen's Printer, Ottawa, p. 479.

34. Smith, W. B., **The New Science,** Ottawa, 1964. Available from W. J. Smith, 50 Oberon, Westcliffe Estates, Ottawa, Canada, K2H 7X8.

CHAPTER 8

1. Gold, T. (Ed). **The Nature of Time.** Cornell University Press, 1967, p. 243.
2. Shklovski and Sagan. **Intelligent Life in the Universe.** Holden-Day, San Francisco, 1966.
3. **International UFO Reporter,** Chicago, Vol. 2, No. 7, 1977.
4. My use of the term "ETI" should not be interpreted as being restricted only to humanoid beings from planets similar to Earth, but can include androids, space animals, etherial beings, or anything else you like, and not native to planet Earth as we know it.
5. Bray, Arthur. **Science, the Public and the UFO.** Bray Book Service, Ottawa, 1967. pp 119-122.

CHAPTER 9

1. Smith, Alson J., **Immortality: The Scientific Evidence,** Prentice-Hall, New York, 1954, pp 138-9.
2. Johnson, Raynor C., **The Imprisoned Splendour,** Harper and Brothers, New York, 1953, p. 110.
3. Smith op cit. p. 140
4. ibid, p. 145.
5. ibid, p. 147.
6. ibid, p. 148.
7. "Psychical Research: The Incredible in Search of Credibility", **Science,** Washington, vol. 181, July 13, 1973.
8. ibid.
9. Smith, op cit. p. 172
10. **National Enquirer.** Lantana, Florida, July 19, 1977.
11. "Psychical Research: The Incredible in Search of Credibility", **Science,** Washington, vol. 181, July 13, 1973.
12. **National Enquirer,** March 29, 1977.
13. David-Neel, Alexandra, **Magic and Mystery in Tibet,** University Books, New Hyde Park, 1965, p. 230.
14. Gauquelin, Michel, **The Cosmic Clocks,** Henry Regnery Co., Chicago, 1967.
15. ibid, Foreword.
16. **Ottawa Journal,** March 2, 1978.

17. Gauquelin, op cit p. 90.

18. ibid. pp 144-45.

19. Leslie Shepard, in Foreword to von Reichenbach, Karl, **The Odic Force: Letters on Od and Magnetism,** University Books, New Hyde Park, 1968.

20. Leslie Shepard, in Foreword to Kilner, Walter J., **The Human Aura,** University Books, New Hyde Park, 1968.

21. ibid.

22. Eden, Jerome, **Orgone Energy,** Exposition Press, New York, 1972.

23. ibid, p. 146.

24. ibid, p. 6.

25. Day, Langston and de la Warr, George, **New Worlds Beyond the Atom,** Devin-Adair, New York, 1963.

26. Los Angeles **Herald Examiner,** February 1, 1977.

27. Eisenbud, Jule, **The World of Ted Serios,** William Morrow & Co., New York, 1967.

28. Puharich, Andrija, **Uri,** Anchor Press/Doubleday, New York, 1974.

29. Crookall, Robert, **Out-of-the-Body Experiences,** University Books, New Hyde Park, 1970, pp 20-21.

30. ibid, p. 22.

31. I Corinthians, XV, 44.

32. Crookall, op cit. p. 35.

33. Fox, Oliver, **Astral Projection: A Record of Out-of-the-Body Experiences,** University Books, New Hyde Park, 1962.

34. Moody, Raymond, **Life After Life,** Bantam Books, New York, 1975.

35. ibid, p. 85.

36. ibid, p. 15.

37. ibid, p. 21.

38. ibid, p. 22.

39. ibid, p. 44.

40. ibid, p. 45.

41. ibid, p. 45.

42. ibid, p. 46.

43. ibid, p. 46.

44. ibid, p. 99.

45. ibid, p. 176.

46. ibid, pp. 87-88.

47. Moody, Raymond, **Reflections on Life after Life,** Bantam/ Mockingbird, Covington, Georgia, 1977.

48. **Ottawa Citizen,** August 3, 1977.

49. Plato, **The Republic,** Book X p. 407, National Library Co., New York Edition Deluxe.

50. Evans-Wentz, W.Y. Ed., **The Tibetan Book of the Dead,** Oxford University Press, London, 1960.

51. Smith, op cit. p. 153.

52. Smith op cit.

53. Graham, Billy, **Angels: God's Secret Agents,** Doubleday & Co., Garden City, 1975.

54. ibid, p. 18.

55. ibid, p. 27.

56. ibid, p. 30.

57. Wilson, Clifford, **Crash Go the Chariots,** Lancer Books, New York, 1972.

58. Wilson, Clifford, **UFOs and their Mission Impossible,** New American Library of Canada, Toronto, 1975.

59. Wilson, Clifford, **Crash Go the Chariots,** pp 7-8.

60. Ravenscroft, Trevor, **The Spear of Destiny,** G.P. Putnams, New York, 1973.

61. Kirk, Robert, **The Secret Commonwealth of Elves, Fawns and Fairies,** Eneas MacKay, Stirling, Scotland, 1933.

62. Evans-Wentz, W.Y., **The Fairy Faith In Celtic Countries,** University Books, New Hyde Park, 1966.

63. ibid, p.280.

64. Hodson, Geoffrey, **The Kingdom of the Gods,** Theosophical Publishing House, Madras, India, 1972.

65. Gardner, E.L., **Fairies: The Cottingley Photographs and Their Sequel,** 4th ed., Theosophical Publishing House, London, 1972.

66. **Winnipeg Free Press,** November 3, 1972.

67. Hoyle, Fred, **The New Face of Science,** New American Library Inc., New York, 1971.

68. Bray, Arthur, **Science the Public and the UFO,** Bray Book Service, Ottawa, 1967.

69. **Science,** vol. 197, August 12, 1977.

70. **KRONOS,** vol. 3, No. 1, Fall 1977.

71. Stannard, F.R., "Symmetry of the Time Axis", **Nature,** London, vol. 211, No. 5050, August 13, 1966, pp 693-695.

72. Hynek, J.A. and Vallee, Jacques, **The Edge of Reality,** Henry Regnery Co., Chicago, 1975.

CHAPTER 10

1. Layne, Meade, **The Coming of the Guardians,** Third Ed., Borderland Sciences Research Association, San Diego, 1957.

2. Wilson, Clifford, **UFOs and Their Mission Impossible,** New American Library of Canada Ltd., Toronto, 1975, p. 156.

3. Vallee, Jacques, **The Psycho-Physical Nature of UFO Reality: A Speculative Framework,** Proceedings of a Symposium "Thesis—Antithesis", American Institute of Aeronautics and Astronautics, Sept. 27, 1975.

4. Layne, op cit.

5. Keel, John A., **The Eighth Tower,** New American Library of Canada, Scarborough, 1977, p. 26.

6. Clark, Adrian V., **Cosmic Mysteries of the Universe,** Parker Publishing Co., West Nyack, N.Y. 1968.

7. Puharich, Andrija, **URI: A Journal of the Mystery of Uri Geller,** Bantam Books, New York, 1975.

8. Constable, Trevor James, **The Cosmic Pulse of Life,** Merlin Press, Santa Ana, 1976.

9. James, Trevor, **They Live in the Sky,** New Age Publishing Co., Los Angeles, 1958.

10. Holiday, F.W., **The Dragon and the Disc,** W.W. Norton Co., New York, 1973.

11. Wilson, op cit. p. 90.

12. Wilson, op cit. pp 92-93.

13. Vallee, Jacques, **Passport to Magonia,** Henry Regnery Co., Chicago, 1969.

14. ibid p. 57.

15. Vallee, Jacques, **The Invisible College,** E.P. Dutton, New York, 1975, p. 14.

16. Shepard, Leslie, in Foreword to **The Fairy Faith in Celtic Countries.** University Books, New Hyde Park, 1966.

17. Schwarz, B.E. "The Man-in-Black Syndrome", **Flying Saucer Review,** London, vol. 23, No. 4, 1977, p. 9.

18. James, op cit. pp. 269-270.

ANNEX 1

1. Lecture presented at a meeting of the American Society of Newspaper Editors in Washington, D.C. on April 22, 1966, as published in "Unidentified Flying Objects—Greatest Scientific Problem of our Times" by Pittsburg Sub-Committee of NICAP, 1967.
2. Hearings before the Committee on Science and Astronautics, U.S. House of Representatives, Ninetieth Congress, Second Session, July 29, 1968.
3. **Electronic News,** January 16, 1967.
4. **The UFO Investigator,** NICAP, Washington, D.C. Vol. IV, January-February, 1968.
5. **Montreal Gazette,** December 16, 1967.
6. Hearings before the Committee on Science and Astronautics, July 29, 1968, p. 119.
7. **Ottawa Citizen,** April 18, 1966.
8. **Aids to Identification of Flying Objects,** U.S. Government Printing Office, 1968, question 16, p. 30.
9. Ibid, Question 14, p. 30.
10. Hearings before the Committee on Science and Astronautics, July 29, 1968, p. 26.
11. **Ottawa Citizen,** July 31, 1968.
12. Bray, Arthur, **Science, the Public and the UFO,** Bray Book Service, Ottawa, 1967.
13. Friedman, Herbert, "The X-Ray Universe", **Earth in Space,** Voice of America Forum Lectures, 1968, p. 277.
14. Bowhill, S.A. "The Ionized Atmosphere", **Earth in Space,** Voice of America Forum Lectures, 1968, pp. 119-120.
15. Cameron, A.G.W., **Interstellar Communication,** W.A. Benjamin, New York, 1963, pp. 121 ff.
16. Tyler, Steven, **Are the Invaders Coming?** Tower Publications Inc., New York, 1968, p. 29.
17. Shklovski & Sagan, **Intelligent Life in the Universe,** Holden-Day, San Francisco, 1966, pp. 362-376.
18. Hearings before the Committee on Science and Astronautics, July 29, 1968, p. 190.
19. Project Bluebook Report No. 8.
20. Official Report, **Unidentified Flying Objects,** Hearing by Committee on Armed Forces of the House of Representatives, Eighty-Ninth Congress, Second Session, April 5, 1966, p. 5995.
21. McDonald, James A. "A Need for an International Study of UFOs", **Flying Saucer Review,** London, Vol. 14, No. 2, 1968, p. 11.
22. **Science,** Vol. 161, July 26, 1968, p. 339.
23. **Scientific Research,** May 13, 1968, p. 12.

24. Saunders, David and Harkins, R. Roger, **UFOs? Yes!** New American Library of Canada, 1968.
25. Smith, W.B., **Project Magnet Report,** 1953 or 1954.
26. **Toronto Star,** October 10, 1968.
27. **Hansard,** December 12, 1968, pp. 3900 and 3901.
28. **UFO Investigator,** Vol. IV, No. 5, March 1968, p. 6.
29. Barnett, Lincoln, **The Universe and Dr. Einstein**, Signet Books, New York, 1965, p. 73.
30. Bernhard, Robert "On the Road with David Green — Campaigning for a New Theory", **Scientific Research**, May 13, 1968, p. 33.
31. Hearings before the Committee on Science and Astronautics, July 29, 1968.
32. McDonald, James E. "A Need for an International Study of UFOs", **Flying Saucer Review**, London, Vol. 14, No. 2, 1968, p. 11.
33. **Science**, November 4, 1966.
34. **73 Magazine**, Vol. XLVII, No. 4, April 1968, p.4.
35. **Mechanical Engineering**, July 1968, American Society of Mechanical Engineers, New York.
36. Gold, T. (Ed), **The Nature of Time**, Cornell University Press, 1967.

Government (of Canada), 48, 56, 62, 66, 67, 69, 71, 74, 87, 114, 141
Graham, Dr. Billy, 93
Green, Dr. David, 132
Green, Dr. Lawrence, 83
Grudge, Project, 124, 125

Halliday, Dr. Ian, 49
Harder, Dr. James A., 117
H-bomb, 59
Health & Welfare, Dept. of, 24
heaven, 93
Herzberg, Dr. Gerhard, 84
Hill, Barney & Betty, 19, 20
Hitler, Adolf, 94, 96
House of Commons, 25, 60, 74, 130
Hoyle, Sir Fred, 96
Hynek, Dr. J. Allen, 16, 39, 42, 99, 116, 123

Institute for Aerospace Studies, 129

Jacobs, Dr. David M., 37
James, William, 119
Jeans, Sir James, 119, 121

Keyhoe, Donald E., 61
Kilner, Dr. Walter J., 86
Kubler-Ross, Dr. Elizabeth, 89, 91

Lamontagne, Senator, 38
landings, 18, 19, 23
Levine, Norman E., 126
levitation, 83
Lovell, Sir Bernard, 117

Magnet, Project, 48, 57-66, 69-74, 127, 152, 153
Magor, John, 54
Maniwaki, 49
Mars, 124

materialization, 101-103
Mather, Barry, 25
Maxwells' equations, 150
McAll, Dr. Kenneth, 94
McDonald, Dr. James E., 38, 116, 119, 120, 125, 136
McDougall, Dr. William, 82
McIntosh, Dr. Bruce, 22
McNamara, Dr. A.G., 51, 55, 69
Men in Black, 105, 106
Michalak, Stephen, 22-25, 51
Millman, Dr, Peter, 49, 51, 60, 61, 67, 128
Mitchell, Dr. Edgar D., 82, 83
molecular structure, 80, 102
Moody, Dr. Raymond, 89-91
Munroe, Hon. John, 55

NASA, 103
National Defense, Dept. of, See DND
National Research Council, See NRC
Non-Meteoritic Sighting Files, 50-52
NORAD, 52
North American Air Defence Command, See NORAD
NRC, 22, 24, 25, 48-55, 57, 60, 67, 128, 129, 139

Occupants, 20, 21, 23, 29, 104
Od, 85, 86
Orgone energy, 86, 87
Oursler, Will, 138
out-of-the-body experience, 89

Parliament, Members of, 130
Patterns, 138
Patterson, Dr. Gordon, 129
photographic evidence, 18, 55, 118
photography, infrared, 104; Kirlian, 87